BEST EVER
FAT FREE
COOKBOOK

BEST EVER
FAT FREE
COOKBOOK

DELICIOUS FOOD FOR
HEALTHY EATING

Anne Sheasby

SWEET WATER PRESS

First published in 1998 by Sweetwater Press
by arrangement with Anness Publishing Limited

© Anness Publishing Limited 1998

Produced by Anness Publishing Limited
Hermes House
88–89 Blackfriars Road
London SE1 8HA

ISBN 1-58173-025-X

Publisher: Joanna Lorenz
Senior Editor: Linda Fraser
Designers: Sara Kidd, Siân Keogh

Front Cover: Lisa Tai, Designer; Thomas Odulate, Photographer; Helen Trent, Stylist;
Marie-Ange Lapierre, Home Economist

Photographers: Karl Adamson, Edward Allwright, Steve Baxter, James Duncan, Amanda Heywood, Don Last,
Patrick McLeavey, Michael Michaels, Thomas Odulate, Peter Reilly
Recipes: Catherine Atkinson, Carla Capalbo, Kit Chan, Roz Denny, Christine France, Linda Fraser, Shirley Gill,
Christine Ingram, Sue Maggs, Annie Nichols, Maggie Pannell, Laura Washburn, Stephen Wheeler
Home Economists: Kit Chan assisted by Lucy McKelvie, Kathryn Hawkins, Wendy Lee, Jane Stevenson, Elizabeth Wolf-Cohe
Stylists: Madeleine Brehaut, Hilary Guy, Jo Harris, Blake Minton, Thomas Odulate, Kirsty Rawlings, Fiona Tillett

Previously published as part of a larger compendium: *The Ultimate Fat-Free Cookbook*

Printed in Hong Kong/China

1 3 5 7 9 10 8 6 4 2

NOTE
Standard spoon and cup measures are level.

CONTENTS

~

INTRODUCTION

Government warnings, magazines and television constantly bombard us with the message that most of us eat too much fat and that this can be very damaging to our health, leading at best to overweight and at worst to fatal diseases. Yet cutting down on fat is not always easy and you can often end up with bland, unexciting, and, frankly, disappointing meals. This book changes all that. It is packed with irresistible recipes from soups to pancakes and from barbecues to cakes—all low in fat.

Of course, some fat is essential in our diets to ensure that our bodies function properly. However, a regime rich in cream, cheese, butter, and fatty meats is not healthy. Changing our approach to what we eat and how we cook it can, literally, be vital. The right sorts of fat in the right sorts of quantities will soon pay dividends in how you feel and how you look.

The easy-to-follow recipes in this book have been specially developed to fit into modern nutritional guidelines—and to be enjoyable. Each one has at-a-glance nutritional information, so you can instantly check the calories, fat, and saturated fat content. The recipes are very low in fat—all contain less than 5 grams of fat per serving and many have even fewer.

Six chapters offer an extensive collection of recipes to suit all occasions: Soups, Appetizers & Snacks; Midweek Meals; Special Occasions; Vegetables & Salads; Desserts; and Cakes, Bakes & Cookies. In addition, the book starts with useful hints and tips on cooking with fat free and low fat ingredients and techniques. Fat free cooking has never been so painless.

FAT FREE GUIDELINES

The fats in food are made up of blocks of fatty acids and glycerol. Fatty acids are made up of chains of carbon atoms. How these chains are linked defines the type of fat: saturated, polyunsaturated, or monounsaturated. All three types are present, in different proportions, in all the food we eat.

TYPES OF FAT

When carbon atoms in the fatty acids have no free bonds to link with other atoms, the fat is saturated. The body finds it hard to process and stores it as fat. Saturated fats raise cholesterol levels in the bloodstream and this may increase the risk of heart disease. Reducing our intake of saturated fats is the first step toward a healthier diet.

Saturated fats are usually solid at room temperature. Their main sources are animal products, such as meat and butter, but some are found in vegetable products, notably palm and coconut oil. Also, vegetable products that are labeled "hydrogenated vegetable oil" have been processed so that some of the unsaturated fatty acids have been converted to saturated.

Polyunsaturated fats are usually liquid at room temperature. There are two types: omega 6 from vegetable sources, such as sunflower oil and soft margarine, and omega 3 from oily fish, such as mackerel. A small intake of these is essential for health and they are thought to help reduce cholesterol levels.

Monounsaturated fats, too, are usually liquid at room temperature and are mainly of vegetable origin. They are found in foods such as olive oil and almonds, and also oily fish. They are thought to help reduce cholesterol levels.

CUTTING DOWN ON FATS

Fats are a concentrated source of energy, but for a healthy diet, the daily intake should not exceed 30 percent of total calories. Of an average total daily intake of 2, 000 calories, only 600 should be supplied by fats. One gram of fat supplies 9 calories, so the maximum daily intake should be no more than 66.6 grams. Saturated fats should form no more than 10 percent of the total calories.

It is fairly easy to cut down on the most obvious sources of fats, such as butter, cream, full-fat milk and cheese, fatty meat and meat products, pastries and rich cakes. However, you should watch out for "hidden" fats in such products as cookies and nuts, as well as in many canned processed foods. Even lean meats with the fat trimmed may contain as much as 10 percent fat.

REDUCED FAT ALTERNATIVES

• Try replacing butter, margarine, and hard fats with low fat spreads or polyunsaturated margarine. Even better for sandwiches and toast, replace them with fat free spreads, such as reduced sugar preserves, yeast extract, reduced fat soft cheese or fat free mayonnaise. Use polyunsaturated or monounsaturated vegetable oils for cooking. Spray oil helps control how much fat you are using for frying.

• Cut down your intake of high fat meat products, such as pies and pâtés. Replace with reduced fat products, lean meat and fish.

• Consider making your own salad dressings with reduced fat yogurt or ricotta cheese, instead of using full fat mayonnaise or French dressing.

• Replace snacks, such as potato chips and cookies with fresh or dried fruits, vegetable sticks or low fat breadsticks.

• Rather than making gravies with meat cooking juices, use vegetable water or fat-free stock.

• From time to time, substitute tofu for meat in curries and other strong-flavored recipes.

• When serving vegetables, sprinkle them with chopped fresh herbs or ground spices rather than adding a knob of butter.

• Substitute reduced fat or skim milk and milk products for full fat dairy products and use reduced fat yogurt instead of cream.

• When buying canned fish such as tuna, choose it canned in brine rather than in oil.

• Substitute fruit juice, wine, beer or fat free stock for fats when cooking.

• To avoid low fat cooking becoming bland, be imaginative with flavorings, such as herbs, spices, soy sauce and wine.

Left: Many varieties of fish and seafood contain less than 1 gram of fat per 4 oz and they are perfect for fat free cooking methods.

It is worth investing in heavy-based or good quality nonstick pans, as you will find that you require far less fat when cooking.

• Always trim any visible fat and skin from all cuts of meat before cooking.

• When roasting or broiling meat, place it on a rack so that the fat drains off.

• Use heavy-based or nonstick cookware for frying so that you can use the minimum amount of fat. Dry fry meat to brown it when making casseroles and meat sauces.

• Poaching is an easy, delicious and fat free method of cooking chicken and fish.

• Steaming is one of the healthiest ways of cooking vegetables, chicken and fish, with the added bonus of preserving their color and texture.

Above: Pulling off chicken and turkey skin and any loose fat directly underneath it before cooking dramatically reduces its fat content.

LOW-FAT FOODS

The following common foods have less than 1 gram of fat per 4 oz of food:

apples	onions
bananas	oranges
broccoli	peaches
cabbage	pears
carrots	peas
cauliflower	potatoes
cod fillets, raw	red kidney
cornflakes	beans, canned
crab, canned	red lentils,
cucumber	cooked
dried mixed	shrimp
fruit	skim milk
egg white	skim milk soft
grapefruit	cheese
haddock, raw	sugar, white
honey	tomatoes
jam	tuna canned in
lemon sole, raw	brine
lima beans,	yoghurt, low fat
canned	plain
mushrooms	zucchini

SOUPS,
APPETIZERS
& SNACKS

CHICKEN AND PASTA SOUP

INGREDIENTS

Serves 4–6

3¾ cups chicken stock
1 bay leaf
4 scallions, sliced
8oz button mushrooms, sliced
4oz cooked chicken breast
2oz soup pasta
⅔ cup dry white wine
1 tablespoon chopped fresh parsley
salt and black pepper

NUTRITION NOTES

Per portion:

Energy	126Kcals/529kJ
Fat	2.2g
Saturated fat	0.6g
Cholesterol	19mg
Fiber	1.3g

1 Put the stock and bay leaf into a pan and bring to a boil.

2 Add the scallions and mushrooms to the stock.

3 Remove the skin from the chicken and slice the meat thinly, using a sharp knife. Add to the soup and season to taste. Heat thoroughly for 2–3 minutes.

4 Add the pasta, cover and simmer for 7–8 minutes. Just before serving, add the wine and chopped parsley, reheat for 2–3 minutes, then season to taste.

CHICKEN AND COCONUT SOUP

This aromatic soup is rich with coconut milk and intensely flavored with galangal, lemongrass and kafir lime leaves.

INGREDIENTS

Serves 4–6

3 cups coconut milk
2 cups chicken stock
4 lemongrass stalks, bruised and
  chopped
1in section galangal, thinly sliced
10 black peppercorns, crushed
10 kafir lime leaves, torn
11oz boneless chicken, cut into thin
  strips
4oz button mushrooms
2oz canned baby corn
4 tbsp lime juice
about 3 tbsp fish sauce
2 fresh chilies, seeded and chopped,
  chopped scallions, and cilantro
  leaves, to garnish

1 Bring the coconut milk and chicken stock to a boil. Add the lemongrass, galangal, peppercorns and half the kafir lime leaves, reduce the heat and simmer gently for 10 minutes.

2 Strain the stock into a clean pan. Return to the heat, then add the chicken, button mushrooms and baby corn. Simmer for 5–7 minutes, or until the chicken is cooked.

3 Stir in the lime juice, fish sauce to taste and the rest of the lime leaves. Serve hot, garnished with chilies, scallions and cilantro.

NUTRITION NOTES

Per portion:

Energy	125Kcals/528kJ
Fat	3.03g
Saturated fat	1.06g
Cholesterol	32.5mg
Fiber	0.4g

HOT AND SOUR SHRIMP SOUP

This is a classic Thai seafood soup and is probably the most popular and well known soup from Thailand.

INGREDIENTS

Serves 4–6

1 lb jumbo shrimp
4 cups chicken stock
3 lemongrass stalks
10 kafir lime leaves, torn in half
8oz can straw mushrooms, drained
3 tbsp fish sauce
¼ cup lime juice
2 tbsp chopped scallions
1 tbsp cilantro leaves
4 fresh chilies, seeded and chopped
salt and black pepper

1 Shell and devein the shrimp and set aside. Rinse the shrimp shells, place them in a large saucepan with the stock and bring to a boil.

2 Bruise the lemongrass stalks with the blunt edge of a chopping knife and add them to the stock with half the lime leaves. Simmer gently for 5–6 minutes, until the stalks change color and the stock is fragrant.

NUTRITION NOTES

Per portion:

Energy	49Kcals/209kJ
Fat	0.45g
Saturated fat	0.07g
Cholesterol	78.8mg
Fiber	0.09g

3 Strain the stock, return to the saucepan and reheat. Add the mushrooms and shrimp, then cook until the shrimp turn pink. Stir in the fish sauce, lime juice, scallions, cilantro, chilies and the rest of the lime leaves. Taste the soup and adjust the seasoning – it should be sour, salty, spicy and hot.

CREAMY COD CHOWDER

A delicious light version of a classic, this chowder is a tasty combination of smoked fish, vegetables, fresh herbs and milk. To cut the calories and stock even more, use vegetable or fish stock in place of the milk. Serve as a substantial first course or snack, or as a light main meal accompanied by warm crusty whole-wheat bread.

INGREDIENTS

Serves 4–6
12oz smoked cod fillet
1 small onion, finely chopped
1 bay leaf
4 black peppercorns
3¾ cups skim milk
2 tsp cornstarch
7oz canned corn
1 tbsp chopped fresh parsley

1 Skin the fish and put it into a large saucepan with the onion, bay leaf and peppercorns. Pour in the milk.

2 Bring to a boil, then reduce the heat and simmer very gently for 12–15 minutes, or until the fish is just cooked. Do not overcook.

3 Using a slotted spoon, lift out the fish and flake into large chunks. Remove the bay leaf and peppercorns and discard.

4 Blend the cornstarch with 2 tsp cold water and add to the pan. Bring to a boil and simmer for 1 minute or until slightly thickened.

5 Drain the corn and add to the saucepan with the flaked fish and parsley. Reheat gently and serve.

COOK'S TIP
The flavor of the chowder improves if it is made a day in advance. Allow to cool, then chill until just before you plan to serve. Reheat gently. Do not allow the soup to boil, or the fish will disintegrate.

NUTRITION NOTES

Per portion:

Energy	200Kcals/840kJ
Protein	24.71g
Fat	1.23g
Saturated fat	0.32g

ITALIAN VEGETABLE SOUP

The success of this clear soup depends on the quality of the stock, so for the best results be sure you use homemade vegetable stock rather than bouillon cubes.

INGREDIENTS

Serves 4

1 small carrot
1 baby leek
1 celery stalk
2oz green cabbage
3¾ cups vegetable stock
1 bay leaf
1 cup cooked cannellini or
    navy beans
⅕ cup soup pasta, such as tiny shells,
    bows, stars or elbows
salt and black pepper
chopped fresh chives, to garnish

1 Cut the carrot, leek and celery into 2in long julienne strips. Slice the cabbage very finely.

NUTRITION NOTES

Per portion:	
Energy	69Kcals/288kJ
Protein	3.67g
Fat	0.71g
Saturated fat	0.05g
Fiber	2.82g

2 Put the stock and bay leaf into a large saucepan and bring to a boil. Add the carrot, leek and celery, cover and simmer for 6 minutes.

3 Add the cabbage, beans and pasta shapes. Stir, then simmer uncovered for another 4–5 minutes, or until the vegetables and pasta are tender.

4 Remove the bay leaf and season with salt and pepper to taste. Ladle into four soup bowls and garnish with chopped chives. Serve immediately.

CARROT AND CILANTRO SOUP

Nearly all root vegetables make excellent soups as they purée well and have an earthy flavor which complements the sharper flavors of herbs and spices. Carrots are particularly versatile, and this simple soup is elegant in both flavor and appearance.

INGREDIENTS

Serves 6
2 tsp sunflower oil
1 onion, chopped
1 celery stalk, sliced, plus 2–3 leafy
    celery tops
2 small potatoes, chopped
1 lb carrots, preferably young and
    tender, chopped
4 cups chicken stock
2–3 tsp ground coriander
1 tbsp chopped fresh cilantro
1 cup low-fat milk
salt and black pepper

1 Heat the oil in a large flameproof casserole or heavy saucepan and fry the onion over gentle heat for 3–4 minutes, until slightly softened but not browned. Add the celery and potato, cook for a few minutes, then add the carrot. Fry over gentle heat for 3–4 minutes, stirring frequently, and then cover. Reduce the heat even further and cook for about 10 minutes. Shake the pan or stir occasionally so the vegetables do not stick.

2 Add the stock, bring to a boil then partially cover and simmer for another 8–10 minutes, until the carrot and potato are tender.

3 Remove 6–8 tiny celery leaves for a garnish and finely chop about 1 tablespoon of the remaining celery tops. In a small saucepan, dry-fry the ground coriander for 1 minute, stirring constantly. Reduce the heat, add the chopped celery and cilantro and fry for about 1 minute. Set aside.

4 Process the soup in a food processor or blender and pour into a clean saucepan. Stir in the milk, coriander mixture and seasoning. Heat gently, taste and adjust the seasoning. Serve garnished with the reserved celery.

NUTRITION NOTES	
Per portion:	
Energy	76.5Kcals/320kJ
Fat	3.2g
Saturated fat	0.65g
Cholesterol	2.3mg
Fiber	2.2g

COOK'S TIP
For a more piquant flavor, add a little freshly squeezed lemon juice just before serving. The contrast between the orange-colored soup and the green garnish is a feast for the eyes as well as the taste buds.

MELON AND BASIL SOUP

A deliciously refreshing, chilled fruit soup, just right for a hot summer's day. It takes next to no time to prepare, leaving you free to enjoy the sunshine and, even better, it is almost totally fat-free.

INGREDIENTS

Serves 4–6
2 cantaloupes
6 tbsp sugar
¾ cup water
finely grated rind and juice of 1 lime
3 tablespoons shredded fresh basil
fresh basil leaves, to garnish

1 Cut the melons in half across the middle. Scrape out the seeds and discard. Using a melon baller, scoop out 20–24 balls and set aside for the garnish. Scoop out the remaining flesh and place in a blender or food processor. Set aside.

2 Place the sugar, water and lime zest in a small pan over low heat. Stir until dissolved, bring to a boil and simmer for 2–3 minutes. Remove from the heat and allow to cool slightly. Pour half the mixture into the blender or food processor with the melon flesh. Blend until smooth, adding the remaining syrup and lime juice to taste.

3 Pour the mixture into a bowl, stir in the basil and chill. Serve garnished with basil leaves and melon balls.

NUTRITION NOTES

Per portion:
Energy	69Kcals/293.8kJ
Fat	0.14g
Saturated fat	0
Cholesterol	0
Fiber	0.47g

COOK'S TIP
Add the syrup in two stages, because the amount of sugar needed will depend on the sweetness of the melon.

GUACAMOLE WITH CRUDITÉS

This fresh-tasting spicy dip is made using peas instead of the avocados that are traditionally associated with this dish. This version saves on both fat and calories, without compromising taste.

INGREDIENTS

Serves 4–6

2¼ cups frozen peas,
    defrosted
1 garlic clove, crushed
2 scallions, chopped
1 tsp finely grated rind and juice of 1
    lime
½ tsp ground cumin
dash of Tabasco sauce
1 tbsp reduced-fat mayonnaise
2 tbsp chopped cilantro
    or parsley
salt and black pepper
pinch of paprika and lime slices,
    to garnish

For the crudités
6 baby carrots
2 celery stalks
1 red-skinned eating apple
1 pear
1 tbsp lemon or lime juice
6 canned baby corns

2 Add the chopped cilantro or parsley and process for a few more seconds. Spoon into a serving bowl, cover with plastic wrap and chill in the fridge for 30 minutes, to let the flavors develop fully.

3 For the crudités, trim and peel the carrots. Halve the celery stalks lengthwise and trim into sticks, the same length as the carrots. Quarter, core and thickly slice the apple and pear, then dip into the lemon or lime juice. Arrange with the baby corn on a platter.

NUTRITION NOTES

Per portion:

Energy	110Kcals/460kJ
Protein	6.22g
Fat	2.29g
Saturated fat	0.49g
Fiber	6.73g

---

1 Put the peas, garlic clove, scallions, lime rind and juice, cumin, Tabasco sauce, mayonnaise and salt and black pepper into a food processor or a blender for a few minutes and process until smooth.

COOK'S TIP
Serve the guacamole with warmed whole-wheat pita bread.

4 Sprinkle the paprika over the guacamole and garnish with twisted lime slices.

CHILI TOMATO SALSA

This universal dip is great served with absolutely anything and can be made up to 24 hours in advance.

INGREDIENTS

Serves 4
1 shallot, peeled and halved
2 garlic cloves, peeled
handful of fresh basil leaves
1¼ lb ripe tomatoes
2 tsp olive oil
2 green chilies
salt and black pepper

1 Place the shallot and garlic in a food processor with the fresh basil. Blend the shallot, garlic and basil until finely chopped.

2 Halve the tomatoes and add to the food processor. Pulse the machine until the mixture is well blended and coarsely chopped.

3 With the motor running, slowly pour in the olive oil. Add salt and pepper to taste.

NUTRITION NOTES	
Per portion:	
Energy	28Kcals/79kJ
Fat	0.47g
Saturated fat	0.13g
Cholesterol	0
Fiber	1.45g

4 Halve the chilies lengthwise and remove the seeds. Finely slice the chilies across the width into tiny strips and stir into the tomato salsa. Serve at room temperature.

COOK'S TIP
The salsa is best made in the summer when tomatoes are at their best. In winter, use a drained 14oz can of plum tomatoes.

PROSCIUTTO AND PEPPER PIZZAS

The delicious flavors of these
easy pizzas are hard to beat.

INGREDIENTS

Makes 4
½ *loaf crusty Italian bread*
1 red bell pepper, roasted and peeled
1 yellow bell pepper, roasted and
  peeled
4 slices prosciutto, cut into
  thick strips
2oz reduced fat mozzarella cheese
black pepper

NUTRITION NOTES

Per portion:	
Energy	93Kcals/395kJ
Fat	3.25g
Saturated fat	1.49g
Cholesterol	14mg
Fiber	1g

1 Cut the bread into four thick slices
and toast until golden.

2 Cut the roasted peppers into thick
strips and arrange on the toasted
bread with the strips of prosciutto.
Preheat the broiler.

3 Thinly slice the mozzarella and
arrange on top, then grind over
plenty of black pepper. Broil for 2–3
minutes, until the cheese is bubbling.

4 Sprinkle the basil leaves on top and
serve immediately.

MELON WITH WILD STRAWBERRIES

This fragrant, colorful first course is the perfect way to begin a rich meal, because both melons and strawberries are virtually fat-free. Here several varieties of melon are combined with strongly flavored wild or woodland strawberries. If wild strawberries are not available, use ordinary strawberries or raspberries.

INGREDIENTS

Serves 4
1 cantaloupe
1 honeydew melon
2 lb watermelon
6oz wild strawberries
4 sprigs fresh mint, to garnish

NUTRITION NOTES

Per portion:
Energy	42.5Kcals/178.6kJ
Fat	0.32g
Saturated fat	0
Cholesterol	0
Fiber	1.09g

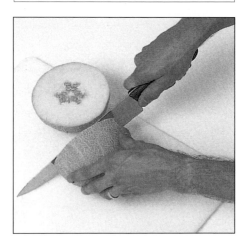

1 Using a large sharp knife, cut all three melons in half.

2 Scoop out the seeds from both the cantaloupe and honeydew melon with a spoon.

3 With a melon scoop, take out as many balls as you can from all three melons. Combine in a large bowl and chill for at least 1 hour.

4 Add the wild strawberries and mix together gently. Spoon out into four stemmed glass dishes.

5 Garnish each of the melon salads with a small sprig of mint and serve immediately.

COOK'S TIP
Ripe melons should give slightly when pressed at the base, and should give off a sweet scent. Buy carefully if you plan to use the fruit on the same day. If one or more varieties of melon aren't available, then substitute another, or buy two or three of the same variety – the salad might not be quite so colorful, but it will taste equally refreshing.

MIDWEEK
MEALS

PASTA WITH CHICKPEA SAUCE

This is a delicious, and very speedy, low fat dish. The quality of canned beans and tomatoes is so good that it is possible to transform them into a very fresh-tasting pasta sauce in minutes. Choose whatever pasta shapes you like, although hollow shapes, such as penne (quills) or shells are particularly good with this sauce.

INGREDIENTS

Serves 6

1 lb penne or other pasta shapes
2 tsp olive oil
1 onion, thinly sliced
1 red bell pepper, seeded and sliced
1 14oz can chopped tomatoes
1 15oz can chickpeas
2 tbsp dry vermouth (optional)
1 tsp dried oregano
1 large bay leaf
2 tbsp capers
salt and black pepper
fresh oregano, to garnish

COOK'S TIP
Choose fresh or dried unfilled pasta for this dish. Whichever you choose, cook it in a large pot of water so that the pasta keeps separate and doesn't stick together. Fresh pasta takes 2–4 minutes to cook and dried pasta 8–10 minutes. Cook pasta until it is *al dente* – firm and neither too hard nor too soft.

NUTRITION NOTES

Per portion:
Energy	268Kcals/1125kJ
Fat	2.0g
Saturated fat	0.5g
Cholesterol	1.3mg
Fiber	4.3g

1 Boil the pasta as instructed on the package, then drain. Meanwhile, heat the oil in a large saucepan and gently fry the onion and pepper for about 5 minutes, stirring occasionally, until softened.

2 Add the tomatoes, chickpeas with their liquid, vermouth (if desired), herbs and capers and stir well.

3 Season to taste and bring to a boil, then simmer for about 10 minutes. Remove the bay leaf and mix in the pasta. Reheat and serve hot, garnished with sprigs of oregano.

TAGLIATELLE WITH MILANESE SAUCE

INGREDIENTS

Serves 4

1 onion, finely chopped
1 celery stalk, finely chopped
1 red bell pepper, seeded and diced
1–2 garlic cloves, crushed
⅔ cup vegetable or chicken stock
1 14oz can tomatoes
1 tbsp tomato paste
2 tsp sugar
1 tsp mixed dried herbs
12oz tagliatelle
1½ cups sliced button mushrooms
4 tbsp dry white wine
4oz lean cooked ham, diced
salt and black pepper
1 tbsp chopped fresh parsley,
   to garnish

1 Put the chopped onion, celery, pepper and garlic into a saucepan. Add the stock, bring to a boil and cook for 5 minutes or until tender.

COOK'S TIP

To reduce the calorie and fat content even more, omit the ham and use corn kernels or cooked broccoli florets instead.

2 Add the tomatoes, tomato paste, sugar and herbs. Season with salt and pepper. Bring to a boil and simmer for 30 minutes, stirring occasionally, until the sauce is thick.

3 Cook the pasta in a large pot of boiling, salted water according to the package instructions, until *al dente*. Drain thoroughly.

4 Put the mushrooms into a pan with the white wine, cover and cook for 3–4 minutes, until the mushrooms are tender and all the wine has been absorbed.

5 Stir the mushrooms and ham into the tomato sauce and reheat gently over low heat.

6 Transfer the pasta to a warmed serving dish and spoon on the sauce. Garnish with parsley.

NUTRITION NOTES

Per portion:

Energy	405Kcals/1700kJ
Fat	3.5g
Saturated fat	0.8g
Cholesterol	17mg
Fiber	4.5g

MUSHROOM AND OKRA CURRY

This simple but delicious curry with its fresh gingery mango relish is best served with plain basmati rice.

INGREDIENTS

Serves 4

4 garlic cloves, coarsely chopped
1in piece fresh ginger, peeled and coarsely chopped
1–2 red chilies, seeded and chopped
¾ cup cold water
1 tbsp sunflower oil
1 tsp coriander seeds
1 tsp cumin seeds
1 tsp ground cumin
2 cardamom pods, seeds removed and crushed
pinch of ground turmeric
1 14oz can chopped tomatoes
1 lb mushrooms, quartered if large
8oz okra, trimmed and cut into ½ in slices
2 tbsp chopped cilantro
basmati rice, to serve

For the mango relish

1 large ripe mango, about 1¼ lb
1 small garlic clove, crushed
1 onion, finely chopped
2 tsp grated fresh ginger
1 fresh red chili, seeded and finely chopped
pinch of salt and sugar

2 Add the rest of the relish ingredients to the mashed mango, mix well and set aside.

1 For the mango relish, peel the mango and then cut off the fruit from the pit. Put the mango into a bowl and mash with a fork, or use a food processor.

3 Place the garlic, ginger, chilies and 3 tbsp of the water into a blender and blend until smooth. Heat the sunflower oil in a large pan. Add the coriander and cumin seeds and allow them to sizzle for a few seconds. Add the ground cumin, cardamom and turmeric and cook for 1 more minute.

4 Add the paste from the blender, the tomatoes, remaining water, mushrooms and okra. Stir to mix well and bring to a boil. Reduce the heat, cover and simmer for 5 minutes. Uncover, turn up the heat slightly and cook for another 5–10 minutes, until the okra is tender. Stir in the cilantro and serve with rice and the mango relish.

NUTRITION NOTES	
Per portion:	
Energy	139Kcals/586kJ
Fat	4.6g
Saturated fat	0.63g
Cholesterol	0
Fiber	6.96g

LENTIL BOLOGNESE

A really useful sauce to serve with pasta, as a pancake stuffing or even as a protein-packed sauce for vegetables.

INGREDIENTS

Serves 6
3 tbsp olive oil
1 onion, chopped
2 garlic cloves, crushed
2 carrots, coarsely grated
2 celery stalks, chopped
⅔ cup red lentils
1 14oz can chopped tomatoes
2 tbsp tomato paste
2 cups stock
1 tbsp fresh marjoram, chopped, or
   1 tsp dried marjoram
salt and black pepper

1 Heat the oil in a large saucepan and gently fry the onion, garlic, carrots and celery for about 5 minutes, until they are soft.

NUTRITION NOTES

Per portion:	
Energy	103Kcals/432kJ
Fat	2.19g
Saturated fat	0.85g
Fiber	2.15g

2 Add the lentils, tomatoes, tomato paste, stock, marjoram and seasoning to the pan.

3 Bring the mixture to a boil, then partially cover with a lid and simmer for 20 minutes, until thick and soft. Use the sauce as required.

COOK'S TIP
You can easily reduce the fat in this recipe by using less olive oil, or substituting a little of the stock and cooking the vegetables over low heat in a non-stick frying pan until they are soft.

VEGETARIAN CASSOULET

Every town in southwest France has its own version of this popular classic. Warm French bread is all that you need to accompany this hearty low fat vegetable version.

INGREDIENTS

Serves 4–6

2 cups dried navy beans
1 bay leaf
2 onions
3 whole cloves
2 garlic cloves, crushed
1 tsp olive oil
2 leeks, thickly sliced
12 baby carrots
4oz button mushrooms
1 14oz can chopped tomatoes
1 tbsp tomato paste
1 tsp paprika
1 tbsp chopped fresh thyme
2 tbsp chopped fresh parsley
2 cups fresh white
  bread crumbs
salt and black pepper

NUTRITION NOTES

Per portion:

Energy	325Kcals/1378kJ
Fat	3.08g
Saturated Fat	0.46g
Cholesterol	0
Fiber	15.68g

COOK'S TIP

If you're short of time, use canned navy beans – you'll need two 14oz cans. Drain, reserving the bean juices and bring up to 1²/₃ cups with vegetable stock.

1 Soak the beans overnight in plenty of cold water. Drain and rinse under cold running water. Put them in a saucepan with 7½ cups of cold water and the bay leaf. Bring to a boil and cook rapidly for 10 minutes.

2 Peel one of the onions and spike with the cloves. Add to the beans, then reduce the heat. Cover and simmer gently for 1 hour, until the beans are almost tender. Drain, reserving the stock but discarding the bay leaf and onion.

3 Chop the remaining onion and put it into a large flameproof casserole together with the crushed garlic and olive oil. Cook gently for 5 minutes, or until softened.

4 Preheat the oven to 325°F. Add the leeks, carrots, mushrooms, chopped tomatoes, tomato paste, paprika and thyme to the casserole, then pour in about 1²/₃ cups of the reserved stock.

5 Bring to a boil, cover and simmer gently for 10 minutes. Stir in the cooked beans and parsley. Season to taste with salt and pepper.

6 Sprinkle the bread crumbs over the top and bake uncovered for 35 minutes, or until the topping is golden brown and crisp.

TURKEY AND TOMATO HOT POT

Here, turkey is turned into tasty meatballs in a rich tomato sauce.

INGREDIENTS

Serves 4
1 slice white bread, crusts removed
2 tbsp skim milk
1 garlic clove, crushed
1/2 tsp caraway seeds
8oz ground turkey
1 egg white
1 1/2 cups chicken stock
1 14oz can tomatoes
1 tbsp tomato paste
1/2 cup quick-cooking rice
salt and black pepper
fresh basil, to garnish
carrot and zucchini ribbons, to serve

1 Cut the bread into small cubes and put into a mixing bowl. Sprinkle over the milk and allow to soak for 5 minutes.

2 Add the garlic clove, caraway seeds, turkey and seasoning to the bread. Stir well.

3 Whisk the egg white until stiff, then fold, half at a time, into the turkey mixture. Chill for 10 minutes.

4 While the turkey mixture is chilling, put the stock, tomatoes and tomato paste into a large saucepan and bring to a boil.

5 Add the rice, stir and cook briskly for about 5 minutes. Turn the heat down to a gentle simmer.

6 Meanwhile, shape the turkey mixture into 16 small balls. Carefully drop them into the tomato stock and simmer for another 8–10 minutes, or until both the turkey balls and rice are cooked. Garnish with basil, and serve with carrot and zucchini ribbons.

COOK'S TIPS
To make carrot and zucchini ribbons, cut the vegetables lengthwise into thin strips using a vegetable peeler, and blanch or steam until lightly cooked.

Lean ground turkey is low in fat and is a good source of protein. It makes an ideal base for this tasty low-fat supper dish. Use ground chicken in place of turkey for an appetizing alternative.

NUTRITION NOTES
Per portion:

Energy	190Kcals/798kJ
Protein	18.04g
Fat	1.88g
Saturated fat	0.24g
Fiber	10.4g

MACARONI AND CHEESE WITH TURKEY

A tasty low fat alternative to macaroni and cheese, the addition of smoked turkey bacon makes this dish a family favorite. Serve with warm Italian bread and a mixed green salad.

NUTRITION NOTES

Per portion:

Energy	152Kcals/637kJ
Fat	2.8g
Saturated fat	0.7g
Cholesterol	12mg
Fiber	1.1g

INGREDIENTS

Serves 4

1 medium onion, chopped
⅔ cup vegetable or chicken stock
2 tbsp low fat margarine
3 tbsp all-purpose flour
¼ cup skim milk
2oz reduced fat Cheddar
   cheese, grated
1 tsp dry mustard
8oz macaroni
4 turkey bacon strips, cut in half
2–3 firm tomatoes, sliced
a few fresh basil leaves
1 tbsp grated Parmesan cheese
salt and black pepper

1 Put the chopped onion and stock into a nonstick frying pan. Bring to a boil, stirring occasionally, and cook for 5–6 minutes or until the stock has reduced entirely and the onion is transparent.

2 Put the margarine, flour, milk and seasoning into a saucepan and whisk together over the heat until thickened and smooth. Set aside and add the cheese, mustard and onion.

3 Cook the macaroni in a large pot of boiling, salted water according to the instructions on the package. Preheat the broiler. Drain the macaroni thoroughly and stir into the sauce. Transfer to a shallow ovenproof dish.

4 Arrange the turkey bacon and tomatoes overlapping on top of the macaroni and cheese. Tuck in the basil leaves, then sprinkle with Parmesan and broil to lightly brown the top.

THAI CHICKEN AND VEGETABLE STIR-FRY

INGREDIENTS

Serves 4

1 piece lemongrass (or the rind of
  ½ lemon)
½in piece fresh ginger
1 large garlic clove
2 tbsp sunflower oil
10oz lean chicken
½ red bell pepper, seeded and sliced
½ green bell pepper, seeded and sliced
4 scallions, chopped
2 medium carrots, cut into matchsticks
4oz thin green beans
1oz peanuts, lightly crushed
2 tbsp oyster sauce
pinch of sugar
salt and black pepper
cilantro leaves, to garnish
steamed rice, to serve

NUTRITION NOTES

Per portion:

Energy	106Kcals/449kJ
Fat	2.05g
Saturated fat	1.10g
Cholesterol	1.10mg
Fiber	109g

1 Thinly slice the lemongrass or lemon rind. Peel and chop the ginger and garlic. Heat the oil in a frying pan over high heat. Add the lemongrass or lemon rind, ginger and garlic, and stir-fry for 30 seconds, until brown.

2 Add the chicken and stir-fry for 2 minutes. Then add all the vegetables and stir-fry for 4–5 minutes, until the chicken is cooked and the vegetables are almost cooked.

3 Finally, stir in the peanuts, oyster sauce, sugar and seasoning to taste. Stir-fry for another minute to blend the flavors. Serve immediately, sprinkled with the cilantro leaves and accompanied by steamed rice.

COOK'S TIP
Make this quick supper dish a little hotter by adding more fresh ginger, if desired.

TUNA AND MIXED VEGETABLE PASTA

INGREDIENTS

Serves 4
2 tsp olive oil
1½ cups button
  mushrooms, sliced
1 garlic clove, crushed
½ red bell pepper, seeded and chopped
1 tbsp tomato paste
1¼ cups tomato juice
1 cup frozen peas
1–2 tbsp drained pickled
  green peppercorns, crushed
12oz whole-wheat pasta shapes
1 7oz can tuna packed in water,
  drained
6 scallions, sliced diagonally

1 Heat the oil in a pan and gently saute the mushrooms, garlic and pepper until softened. Stir in the tomato paste, then add the tomato juice, peas and some or all of the crushed peppercorns, depending on how spicy you like the sauce. Bring to a boil, lower the heat and simmer.

2 Bring a large saucepan of lightly salted water to a boil and cook the pasta for about 12 minutes (or according to the instructions on the package), until just tender. When the pasta is almost ready, add the tuna to the sauce and heat through gently. Stir in the scallions. Drain the pasta, turn it into a heated bowl and pour on the sauce. Toss to mix. Serve at once.

NUTRITION NOTES	
Per portion:	
Energy	354Kcals/1514kJ
Fat	4.5g
Saturated fat	0.67g
Cholesterol	22.95mg
Fiber	10.35g

SWEET AND SOUR FISH

White fish is high in protein, vitamins and minerals, but low in fat. Serve this tasty, nutritious dish with brown rice and stir-fried cabbage or spinach for a delicious lunch.

INGREDIENTS

Serves 4
4 tbsp cider vinegar
3 tbsp light soy sauce
¼ cup granulated sugar
1 tbsp tomato paste
1½ tbsp cornstarch
1 cup water
1 green bell pepper, seeded and sliced
1 8oz can pineapple chunks
  in juice
8oz tomatoes, peeled and chopped
2 cups sliced button mushrooms
1½ lb thick haddock fillets,
  skinned
salt and black pepper

1 Preheat the oven to 350°F. Combine the vinegar, soy sauce, sugar and tomato paste in a saucepan. Put the cornstarch in a cup, stir in the water, then add the mixture to the saucepan, stirring well. Bring to a boil, stirring constantly until thickened. Lower the heat and simmer the sauce for 5 minutes.

2 Add the green pepper, canned pineapple chunks (with juice) and tomatoes to the pan and stir well. Mix in the mushrooms and heat through. Season to taste with salt and pepper.

3 Place the fish in a single layer in a shallow ovenproof dish, spoon on the sauce and cover with foil. Bake for 15–20 minutes, until the fish is tender. Serve immediately.

NUTRITION NOTES	
Per portion:	
Energy	255Kcals/1070kJ
Fat	2g
Saturated fat	0.5g
Cholesterol	61mg

HOT SPICY SHRIMP WITH PASTA

This low fat shrimp sauce tossed with hot pasta is an ideal supper-time dish. Add less or more chili depending on how hot you like your food.

INGREDIENTS

Serves 4–6

8oz large shrimp, cooked and peeled
1–2 garlic cloves, crushed
finely grated rind of 1 lemon
1 tbsp lemon juice
¼ tsp red chili paste or 1 large pinch of chili powder
1 tbsp light soy sauce
5oz smoked turkey bacon strips
1 shallot or small onion, finely chopped
4 tbsp dry white wine
8oz campanelle or other pasta shapes
4 tbsp fish stock
4 firm ripe tomatoes, peeled, seeded and chopped
2 tbsp chopped fresh parsley
salt and black pepper

NUTRITION NOTES

Per portion:

Energy	331Kcals/1388kJ
Fat	2.9g
Saturated fat	0.6g
Cholesterol	64mg
Fiber	3.2g

COOK'S TIP

To save time later, the shrimp and marinade ingredients can be mixed together, covered and chilled in the fridge overnight, until ready to use.

1 In a glass bowl, mix the shrimp with the garlic, lemon rind and juice, chili paste and soy sauce. Season with salt and pepper, cover and marinate for at least 1 hour.

2 Broil the turkey bacon strips, then cut them into ¼ in dice.

3 Put the shallot or onion and white wine into a pan, bring to a boil, cover and cook for 2–3 minutes, or until they are tender and the wine has reduced by half.

4 Cook the pasta according to the package instructions in a large pot of boiling, salted water until *al dente*. Drain thoroughly.

5 Just before serving, put the shrimp with its marinade into a large frying pan, bring to a boil quickly and add the smoked turkey bacon and fish stock. Heat thoroughly for 1 minute.

6 Add to the pasta with the chopped tomatoes and parsley, toss quickly and serve immediately.

HERBED FISHCAKES WITH LEMON SAUCE

The wonderful flavor of fresh herbs makes these fishcakes the catch of the day.

INGREDIENTS

Serves 4

12oz potatoes, coarsely chopped
5 tbsp skim milk
12oz haddock
  fillets, skinned
1 tbsp lemon juice
1 tbsp horseradish sauce
2 tbsp chopped fresh parsley
flour, for dusting
2 cups fresh whole-wheat bread crumbs
salt and black pepper
parsley sprigs, to garnish
sugar snap peas or snow peas and a
  sliced tomato and onion salad,
  to serve

For the lemon and chive sauce
thinly pared rind and juice of
  ½ small lemon
½ cup dry white wine
2 thin slices of fresh ginger
2 tsp cornstarch
2 tbsp chopped fresh chives

NUTRITION NOTES

Per portion:

Energy	232Kcals/975kJ
Protein	19.99g
Fat	1.99g
Saturated fat	0.26g
Fiber	3.11g

COOK'S TIP
Dry white wine is a tasty fat-free basis for this herb sauce. Try using cider as an alternative to wine, for a change.

1 Cook the potatoes in a large saucepan of boiling water for 15–20 minutes. Drain and mash with the milk and season to taste.

2 Purée the fish together with the lemon juice and horseradish sauce in a blender or food processor. Mix with the potatoes and parsley.

3 With floured hands, shape the mixture into eight fishcakes and coat with the breadcrumbs. Chill in the fridge for 30 minutes.

4 Preheat the grill to medium and cook the fishcakes for 5 minutes on each side, until browned.

5 To make the sauce, cut the lemon rind into julienne strips and put into a large saucepan together with the lemon juice, wine and ginger. Season to taste with salt and pepper.

6 Simmer, uncovered, for about 6 minutes. Blend the cornstarch with 1 tbsp of cold water, add to the pan and simmer until clear. Stir in the chives immediately before serving.

7 Serve the sauce hot with the fishcakes, garnished with parsley sprigs and accompanied by peas and a tomato and onion salad.

MEDITERRANEAN FISH FILLETS

These low fat fish fillets are nicely complemented by boiled potatoes, broccoli and carrots.

─ INGREDIENTS ─

Serves 4

4 white fish fillets, about
   5oz each
⅓ cup fish stock or dry white wine (or
   a mixture of the two), for poaching
1 bay leaf, a few black peppercorns
   and a strip of pared lemon rind, for
   flavoring
chopped fresh parsley, to garnish

For the tomato sauce

1 14oz can chopped tomatoes
1 garlic clove, crushed
1 tbsp pastis or other anise-
   flavored liqueur
1 tbsp drained capers
12–16 pitted black olives
salt and black pepper

1 To make the sauce, place the chopped tomatoes, garlic, pastis, capers and olives in a saucepan. Season to taste with salt and pepper and cook over low heat for about 15 minutes, stirring occasionally.

2 Place the fish in a frying pan, pour over the stock and/or wine and add the bay leaf, peppercorns and lemon rind. Cover and simmer for 10 minutes or until it flakes easily.

3 Using a slotted spoon, transfer the fish into a heated dish. Strain the stock into the tomato sauce and boil to reduce slightly. Season the sauce, pour it over the fish and serve immediately, sprinkled with the chopped parsley.

> **COOK'S TIP**
> Remove skin from cutlets and reduce the quantity of olives to reduce calories and fat. Use 1 lb fresh tomatoes, skinned and chopped, in place of the canned tomatoes.

─ NUTRITION NOTES ─

Per portion:

Energy	165Kcals/685kJ
Fat	3.55g
Saturated fat	0.5g
Cholesterol	69mg

PASTA PRIMAVERA

You can use any mixture of fresh, young spring vegetables to make this delicately flavored pasta dish.

INGREDIENTS

*8oz thin asparagus spears, chopped
    in half*
4oz snow peas, ends removed
*4oz canned baby corn or fresh corn
    kernels*
8oz whole baby carrots, trimmed
*1 small red bell pepper, seeded and
    chopped*
8 scallions, sliced
8oz torchietti or other pasta shapes
⅔ cup low fat cottage cheese
⅔ cup low fat yogurt
1 tbsp lemon juice
1 tbsp chopped parsley
1 tbsp chopped chives
skim milk (optional)
salt and black pepper
sun-dried tomato bread, to serve

1 Cook the asparagus spears in a pan of boiling, salted water for 3–4 minutes. Add the snow peas halfway through the cooking time. Drain and rinse both under cold water to stop further cooking.

2 Cook the corn, carrots, red pepper and scallions in the same way until tender. Drain and rinse.

3 Cook the pasta in a large pot of boiling, salted water according to the packet instruction, until *al dente*. Drain thoroughly.

4 Put the cottage cheese, yogurt, lemon juice, parsley, chives and seasoning into a food processor or blender and process until smooth. Thin the sauce with skim milk, if necessary. Put into a large pan with the pasta and vegetables, heat gently and toss carefully. Serve immediately with sun-dried tomato bread.

NUTRITION NOTES

Per portion:

Energy	320Kcals/1344kJ
Fat	3.1g
Saturated fat	0.4g
Cholesterol	3mg
Fiber	6.2g

SPECIAL
OCCASIONS

TOFU AND GREEN BEAN CURRY

This exotic curry is simple and quick to make. This recipe uses beans and mushrooms, but you can use almost any kind of vegetable, such as eggplant, bamboo shoots or broccoli.

INGREDIENTS

Serves 4
1½ cups coconut milk
1 tbsp red curry paste
3 tbsp fish sauce
2 tsp sugar
8oz button mushrooms
4oz green beans, trimmed
6oz tofu, rinsed and cut into
  ¾in cubes
4 kafir lime leaves, torn
2 red chilies, seeded and sliced
cilantro leaves, to garnish

NUTRITION NOTES

Per portion:	
Energy	100Kcals/420kJ
Fat	3.36g
Saturated fat	0.48g
Cholesterol	0
Fiber	1.35g

1 Put about one third of the coconut milk in a wok or saucepan. Cook until it starts to separate and an oily sheen appears.

2 Add the red curry paste, fish sauce and sugar to the coconut milk. Mix together thoroughly.

3 Add the mushrooms. Stir and cook for 1 minute.

4 Stir in the rest of the coconut milk and bring back to a boil.

> **COOK'S TIP**
> Use 1–2 tsp hot chili powder, if fresh red chilies aren't available. When preparing fresh chilies, wear rubber gloves and wash hands, work surfaces and utensils thoroughly afterwards. Chilies contain volatile oils which can irritate and burn sensitive areas, especially eyes.

5 Add the green beans and cubes of tofu and simmer gently for another 4–5 minutes.

6 Stir in the kafir lime leaves and chilies. Serve garnished with the cilantro leaves.

RATATOUILLE PANCAKES

These pancakes are made slightly thicker than usual to hold the juicy vegetable filling. By using cooking spray, you can control the amount of fat you are using and keep it to a minimum.

INGREDIENTS

Serves 4
⅔ cup all-purpose flour
pinch of salt
¼ cup quick-cooking oatmeal
1 egg
1¼ cups skim milk
nonstick cooking spray
mixed salad, to serve

For the filling
1 large eggplant, cut into
  1in cubes
1 garlic clove, crushed
2 medium zucchini, sliced
1 green bell pepper, seeded and sliced
1 red bell pepper, seeded and sliced
5 tbsp vegetable stock
1 7oz can chopped tomatoes
1 teaspoon cornstarch
salt and black pepper

NUTRITION NOTES

Per portion:
Energy	182Kcals/767kJ
Protein	9.36g
Fat	3.07g
Saturated fat	0.62g
Fiber	4.73g

COOK'S TIP
Adding oatmeal to the batter mixture adds flavor, color and texture to the cooked pancakes. If desired, use whole-wheat flour in place of white flour to add extra fiber and flavor.

1 Sift the flour and a pinch of salt into a bowl. Stir in the oats. Make a well in the center, add the egg and half the milk and mix to a smooth batter. Gradually beat in the remaining milk. Cover the bowl and allow to stand for 30 minutes.

2 Spray a 7in heavy pan with cooking spray. Heat the pan, then pour in just enough batter to cover the bottom of the pan thinly. Cook for 2–3 minutes, until the underside is golden brown. Flip over and cook for another 1–2 minutes.

3 Slide the pancake out onto a plate lined with nonstick baking paper. Stack the other pancakes on top as they are made, interleaving each with parchment paper. Keep warm.

4 For the filling, put the eggplant in a colander and sprinkle well with salt. Let stand on a plate for 30 minutes. Rinse thoroughly and drain well.

5 Put the garlic clove, zucchini, peppers, stock and tomatoes into a large saucepan. Simmer uncovered, stirring occasionally, for 10 minutes. Add the eggplant and cook for another 15 minutes. Blend the cornstarch with 2 teaspoons water and stir into the saucepan. Simmer for 2 minutes. Season to taste.

6 Spoon some of the ratatouille mixture into the middle of each pancake. Fold each one in half, then in half again to make a cone shape. Serve hot with a mixed salad.

AUTUMN GLORY

Glorious pumpkin shells summon up the delights of autumn and look too good to throw away, so use one as a serving pot. Pumpkin and pasta make great partners, especially as a main course served from the baked shell.

INGREDIENTS

Serves 4–6
1 pumpkin, about 4–4½ lb
1 onion, sliced
1in piece fresh ginger
1 tbsp extra virgin olive oil
1 zucchini, sliced
1¾ cups sliced mushrooms
1 14oz chopped tomatoes
1 cup pasta shells
2 cups stock
4 tbsp ricotta cheese
2 tbsp chopped fresh basil
salt and black pepper

NUTRITION NOTES

Per portion (for 6):
Energy	140Kcals/588kJ
Fat	4.29g
Saturated fat	1.17g
Cholesterol	2.5mg
Fiber	4.45g

COOK'S TIP
Use reduced-fat or very low fat ricotta cheese to cut the calories and fat. Cook the onion, ginger and pumpkin flesh in 2–3 tbsp vegetable stock in place of the oil, to cut the calories and fat even more.

1 Preheat the oven to 350°F. Cut the top off the pumpkin with a large sharp knife, then scoop out and discard the seeds.

2 Using a small sharp knife and a sturdy tablespoon, extract as much of the pumpkin flesh as possible, then chop it into chunks.

3 Bake the pumpkin shell with its lid on for 45 minutes to 1 hour, until the inside begins to soften.

4 Meanwhile make the filling. Gently fry the onion, ginger and pumpkin chunks in the olive oil for about 10 minutes, stirring occasionally.

5 Add the zucchini and mushrooms and cook for another 3 minutes, then stir in the tomatoes, pasta shells and stock. Season well, bring to a boil, then cover and simmer gently for another 10 minutes.

6 Stir the ricotta cheese and basil into the pasta and spoon the mixture into the pumpkin. (It may not be possible to fit all the filling into the pumpkin shell; serve the rest separately if this is the case.)

PASTA WITH HERBED SCALLOPS

Low-fat ricotta cheese, flavored with mustard, garlic and herbs, makes a deceptively creamy sauce for pasta.

INGREDIENTS

Serves 4
½ cup low-fat ricotta cheese
2 tsp whole-grain mustard
2 garlic cloves, crushed
2–3 tbsp fresh lime juice
4 tbsp chopped fresh parsley
2 tbsp chopped chives
12oz black tagliatelle
12 large bay scallops
4 tbsp white wine
⅔ cup fish stock
salt and black pepper
lime wedges and parsley sprigs,
   to garnish

1 To make the sauce, combine the ricotta cheese, mustard, garlic, lime juice, parsley, chives and seasoning in a mixing bowl.

2 Cook the pasta in a large pot of boiling salted water until *al dente*. Drain thoroughly.

3 Slice the scallops in half horizontally. Put the wine and fish stock into a saucepan and heat to simmering point. Add the scallops and cook very gently for 3–4 minutes at the most. (Don't cook any longer, or they will toughen.)

COOK'S TIP
Black tagliatelle, made with squid ink, is available from Italian delicatessens, but other colors can be used to make this dish – try a mixture of white and green.

4 Remove the scallops. Boil the wine and stock to reduce by half and add the green sauce to the pan. Heat gently to warm, then return the scallops to the pan and cook for 1 minute. Spoon onto the pasta and garnish with lime wedges and parsley.

NUTRITION NOTES

Per portion:
Energy	368Kcals/1561kJ
Fat	4.01g
Saturated fat	0.98g
Cholesterol	99mg
Fiber	1.91g

BAKED FISH IN BANANA LEAVES

Fish that is prepared in this way is particularly succulent and full of flavor. Fillets are used here, rather than whole fish, which is easier for those who don't like to mess with bones. It is a great dish for a barbecue.

INGREDIENTS

Serves 4

1 cup coconut milk
2 tbsp red curry paste
3 tbsp fish sauce
2 tbsp sugar
5 kafir lime leaves, torn
6oz fish fillets, such
  as snapper
6oz mixed vegetables, such as
  carrots or leeks, finely shredded
4 banana leaves or pieces of foil
2 tbsp shredded scallions,
  to garnish
2 red chilies, finely sliced, to garnish

NUTRITION NOTES

Per portion:
Energy	258Kcals/1094kJ
Fat	4.31g
Saturated fat	0.7g
Cholesterol	64.75mg
Fiber	1.23g

COOK'S TIP
Coconut milk is low in calories and fat and so makes an ideal basis for a low fat marinade or sauce. Choose colorful vegetables such as carrots, leeks and red bell pepper, to make the dish more attractive and appealing.

1 Combine the coconut milk, curry paste, fish sauce, sugar and kafir lime leaves in a shallow dish.

2 Marinate the fish in this mixture for 15–30 minutes. Preheat the oven to 400°F.

3 Lay a portion of the mixed vegetables on top of a banana leaf or piece of foil. Place a piece of fish on top with a little of its marinade.

4 Wrap the fish up by turning in the sides and ends of the leaf and secure with toothpicks. (With foil, just pinch the edges together.) Repeat with the rest of the fish.

5 Bake for 20–25 minutes or until the fish is cooked. Alternatively, cook under the broiler or on a barbecue. Just before serving, garnish the fish with a sprinkling of scallions and sliced red chilies.

SEAFOOD SALAD WITH FRAGRANT HERBS

INGREDIENTS

Serves 6

1 cup fish stock or water
12oz squid, cleaned and cut
   into rings
12 uncooked jumbo shrimp, shelled
12 scallops
2oz bean thread noodles, soaked in
   warm water for 30 minutes
½ cucumber, cut into thin sticks
1 lemongrass stalk, finely chopped
2 kafir lime leaves, finely shredded
2 shallots, finely sliced
juice of 1–2 limes
2 tbsp fish sauce
2 tbsp chopped scallions
2 tbsp chopped cilantro leaves
12–15 mint leaves, roughly torn
4 red chilies, seeded and sliced
cilantro sprigs, to garnish

1 Pour the stock or water into a medium saucepan, set over high heat and bring to a boil.

2 Cook each type of seafood separately in the stock. Don't overcook – it takes only a few minutes for each. Remove and set aside.

3 Drain the bean thread noodles and cut them into short lengths, about 2in long. Combine the noodles with the cooked seafood.

4 Add all the remaining ingredients, stir well and serve garnished with cilantro sprigs.

NUTRITION NOTES

Per portion:
Energy	78Kcals/332kJ
Fat	1.12g
Saturated fat	0.26g
Cholesterol	123mg
Fiber	0.37g

COOK'S TIP

Use other prepared seafood, such as mussels and crabmeat, in place of the shrimp or scallops. If fresh chilies are not available, use 2–3 tsp of hot ground chilies or, alternatively, use dried chopped chilies.

SOLE FILLETS BAKED IN A PAPER CASE

INGREDIENTS

Serves 4
*4 sole or flounder fillets, about
  5 ounces each*
½ small cucumber, sliced
4 lemon slices
4 tbsp dry white wine
sprigs of fresh dill, to garnish
potatoes and braised celery, to serve

For the yogurt hollandaise
½ cup low fat plain yogurt
1 tsp lemon juice
2 egg yolks
1 tsp Dijon mustard
salt and black pepper

1 Preheat the oven to 350°F. Cut out four heart shapes from nonstick parchment paper, each about 8 x 6 in.

2 Place a sole fillet on one side of each paper heart. Arrange the cucumber and lemon slices on top of each fillet. Sprinkle with the wine and close the packages by turning the edges of the paper and twisting to secure. Put the packages on a baking sheet and cook for 15 minutes.

3 Meanwhile make the hollandaise. Beat together the yogurt, lemon juice and egg yolks in a double boiler or bowl placed over a saucepan. Cook over simmering water, stirring for about 15 minutes, or until thickened. (The sauce will become thinner after 10 minutes, but will thicken again.)

COOK'S TIP
Make sure that the paper packages are well sealed, so that none of the delicious juices can escape.

4 Remove from the heat and stir in the mustard. Season to taste with salt and pepper. Open the fish packages, garnish with a sprig of dill and serve accompanied with the sauce, new potatoes and braised celery.

NUTRITION NOTES
Per portion:
Energy	185Kcals/779kJ
Protein	29.27g
Fat	4.99g
Saturated fat	1.58g
Fiber	0.27g

THAI BEEF SALAD

A hearty salad of beef, laced with a chili and lime dressing.

INGREDIENTS

Serves 6

6 lean sirloin steaks, 3oz each
1 red onion, finely sliced
1/2 cucumber, finely sliced
   into matchsticks
1 lemongrass stalk, finely chopped
2 tbsp chopped scallions
juice of 2 limes
1–2 tbsp fish sauce
2–4 red chilies, finely sliced, to garnish
cilantro, Chinese mustard cress and
   mint leaves, to garnish

NUTRITION NOTES

Per portion:

Energy	101Kcals/424kJ
Fat	3.8g
Saturated fat	1.7g
Cholesterol	33.4mg
Fiber	0.28g

COOK'S TIP
Round or tenderloin steaks would work just as well in this recipe. Choose good-quality lean steaks and remove and discard any visible fat.

---

1 Broil the sirloin steaks until they are medium-rare, then allow to rest for 10–15 minutes.

2 When cool, thinly slice the beef and put the slices in a large bowl.

3 Add the sliced onion, cucumber matchsticks and lemongrass.

4 Add the scallions. Toss and season with lime juice and fish sauce. Serve at room temperature or chilled, garnished with the chilies, cilantro, mustard cress and mint.

THAI-STYLE CHICKEN SALAD

This salad comes from Chiang Mai, a city in the northeast of Thailand. It's hot and spicy, and wonderfully aromatic. Choose strong-flavored leaves, such as curly endive or arugula, for the salad.

INGREDIENTS

Serves 6

1 lb ground chicken breast
1 lemongrass stalk, finely chopped
3 kafir lime leaves, finely chopped
4 red chilies, seeded and chopped
4 tbsp lime juice
2 tbsp fish sauce
1 tbsp roasted ground rice
2 scallions, chopped
2 tbsp cilantro leaves
mixed salad leaves, cucumber and
    tomato slices, to serve
mint sprigs, to garnish

1 Heat a large nonstick frying pan. Add the ground chicken and cook in a little water.

2 Stir constantly until cooked, which will take about 7–10 minutes.

3 Transfer the cooked chicken to a large bowl and add the rest of the ingredients. Mix thoroughly.

4 Serve on a bed of mixed salad leaves, cucumber and tomato slices, garnished with mint sprigs.

COOK'S TIP
Use sticky (glutinous) rice to make roasted ground rice. Put the rice in a frying pan and dry-roast until golden brown. Remove and grind to a powder with a mortar and pestle or in a food processor. Keep in a glass jar in a cool dry place and use as needed.

NUTRITION NOTES	
Per portion:	
Energy	106Kcals/446kJ
Fat	1.13g
Saturated fat	0.28g
Cholesterol	52.5mg
Fiber	0.7g

FRAGRANT CHICKEN CURRY

In this dish, the mildly spiced sauce is thickened using lentils rather than the traditional onions fried in ghee.

INGREDIENTS

Serves 4–6

½ cup red lentils
2 tbsp mild curry powder
2 tsp ground coriander
1 tsp cumin seeds
2 cups vegetable stock
8 chicken thighs, skinned
8oz fresh shredded spinach, or frozen,
    thawed and well drained
1 tbsp chopped cilantro
salt and black pepper
sprigs of cilantro, to garnish
white or brown basmati rice and
    broiled poppadums, to serve

1 Rinse the lentils under cold running water. Put in a large, heavy saucepan with the curry powder, ground coriander, cumin seeds and vegetable stock.

2 Bring to a boil, then lower the heat. Cover and simmer gently for about 10 minutes.

NUTRITION NOTES

Per portion:
Energy	152Kcals/640kJ
Fat	4.9g
Saturated fat	1.3g
Added Sugar	0
Fiber	2.6g

COOK'S TIP
Lentils are an excellent source of fiber, and add color and texture.

3 Add the chicken and spinach. Replace the cover and simmer gently for another 40 minutes, or until the chicken has cooked.

4 Stir in the chopped cilantro and season to taste. Serve garnished with cilantro and accompanied by the rice and broiled poppadums.

RAGOÛT OF VEAL

If you are looking for a low-calorie dish to treat yourself – or some guests – then this is perfect, and quick, too.

INGREDIENTS

Serves 4

12oz veal cutlets or loin
2 tsp olive oil
10–12 tiny onions, kept whole
1 yellow bell pepper, seeded and cut into eighths
1 orange or red bell pepper, seeded and cut into eighths
3 tomatoes, peeled and quartered
4 fresh basil sprigs
2 tbsp dry vermouth or sherry
salt and black pepper

NUTRITION NOTES

Per portion:
Energy	158Kcals/665.5kJ
Fat	4.97g
Saturated Fat	1.14g
Cholesterol	63mg
Fiber	2.5g

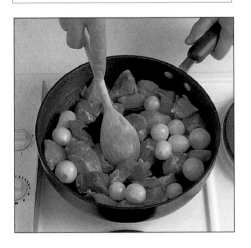

1 Trim off any fat and cut the veal into cubes. Heat the oil in a frying pan and gently stir-fry the veal and onions until browned.

2 After a couple of minutes, add the peppers and tomatoes. Continue stir-frying for another 4–5 minutes.

COOK'S TIP
Lean beef or pork fillet may be used instead of veal, if you prefer. Shallots can replace the onions.

3 Add half the basil leaves, coarsely chopped (keep some for garnish), the vermouth or sherry, and seasoning. Cook, stirring frequently, for another 10 minutes, or until the meat is tender.

4 Sprinkle with the remaining basil leaves and serve hot.

VEGETABLES
& SALADS

POTATO GRATIN

The flavor of Parmesan is wonderfully strong, so a little goes a long way. Leave the cheese out altogether for an almost fat-free dish.

─── INGREDIENTS ───

Serves 4
1 garlic clove
5 large baking potatoes, peeled
3 tbsp freshly grated Parmesan cheese
2½ cups vegetable or chicken stock
pinch of grated nutmeg
salt and black pepper

1 Preheat the oven to 400°F. Halve the garlic clove and rub the cut surface over the base and sides of a large shallow gratin dish.

2 Slice the potatoes very thinly and arrange a third of them in the dish. Sprinkle with a little grated Parmesan cheese, and season with salt and pepper. Pour on some of the stock to prevent the potatoes from discoloring.

3 Continue layering the potatoes and cheese as before, then add the rest of the stock. Sprinkle with the grated nutmeg.

COOK'S TIP
For a potato and onion gratin, thinly slice one medium onion and layer with the potato.

4 Bake in the preheated oven for 1¼–1½ hours, or until the potatoes are tender and the tops well browned.

NUTRITION NOTES	
Per portion:	
Energy	178Kcals/749kJ
Protein	9.42g
Fat	1.57g
Saturated fat	0.30g
Fiber	1.82g

BAKED GARLIC POTATOES

With a low fat topping these would make a superb meal in themselves or could be enjoyed as a nutritious accompaniment to grilled fish or meat.

INGREDIENTS

Serves 4

4 baking potatoes
2 garlic cloves, cut into slivers
4 tbsp low fat ricotta cheese
4 tbsp low fat plain yogurt
2 tbsp snipped chives
6–8 watercress sprigs, finely chopped
(optional)

NUTRITION NOTES

Per portion:	
Energy	195Kcals/815kJ
Fat	3.5g
Saturated fat	2g
Cholesterol	10mg

1 Preheat the oven to 400°F. Slice each potato at about ¼in intervals, cutting not quite to the base, so that they retain their shape. Slip the slivers of the garlic between the cuts in the potatoes.

COOK'S TIP
If available, farmer's cheese or low fat cream cheese are very good substitutes for the ricotta cheese.

2 Place the garlic-filled potatoes in a roasting tin and bake for 1–1¼ hours, or until soft when tested with a knife. Meanwhile, mix the low fat ricotta cheese and yogurt in a bowl, then stir in the snipped chives, along with the watercress, if using.

3 Serve the baked potatoes on individual plates, with a dollop of the yogurt and ricotta cheese mixture on top of each.

POTATO, LEEK AND TOMATO TIAN

INGREDIENTS

Serves 4

1½ lb potatoes
2 leeks, sliced
3 large tomatoes, sliced
a few fresh rosemary sprigs, crushed
1 garlic clove, crushed
1¼ cups vegetable stock
1 tbsp olive oil
salt and black pepper

NUTRITION NOTES

Per portion:	
Energy	180Kcals/740kJ
Fat	3.5g
Saturated fat	0.5g
Cholesterol	0

1 Preheat the oven to 350°F and grease a 5-cup shallow ovenproof dish. Scrub and thinly slice the potatoes. Alternately layer them with the leeks and tomatoes in the dish, sprinkling some rosemary between the layers and ending with a layer of potatoes.

2 Add the garlic to the stock, stir in salt if needed and pepper to taste, then add to the vegetables. Brush the top layer of potatoes with olive oil.

3 Bake for 1¼–1½ hours, until the potatoes are tender and the topping is golden and slightly crisp.

ZUCCHINI IN CITRUS SAUCE

If baby zucchini are unavailable, you can use larger ones, but they should be cooked whole, so that they don't absorb too much water. After cooking, halve them lengthwise and cut into 4-inch lengths. These tender, baby zucchini served in a very low fat sauce make this a tasty and low fat accompaniment to grilled fish fillets.

INGREDIENTS

Serves 4
12oz baby zucchini
4 scallions, finely sliced
1in piece fresh ginger, grated
2 tbsp cider vinegar
1 tbsp light soy sauce
1 tsp light brown sugar
3 tbsp vegetable stock
finely grated rind and juice of ½ lemon
    and ½ orange
1 tsp cornstarch

NUTRITION NOTES	
Per portion:	
Energy	33Kcals/138kJ
Protein	2.18g
Fat	0.42g
Saturated fat	0.09g
Fiber	0.92g

1 Cook the zucchini in lightly salted boiling water for 3–4 minutes or until just tender. Drain well.

2 Meanwhile, put all the remaining ingredients, except the cornstarch, into a small saucepan and bring to a boil. Simmer for 3 minutes.

3 Blend the cornstarch with 2 tsp cold water and add to the sauce. Bring to a boil, stirring constantly, until the sauce has thickened.

4 Pour the sauce over the zucchini and heat gently, shaking the pan to coat them evenly. Transfer to a warmed serving dish and serve.

COOK'S TIP
Use baby corn or eggplant in place of the zucchini for an appetizing change.

ROASTED MEDITERRANEAN VEGETABLES

For a really colorful dish, try these vegetables roasted in olive oil with garlic and rosemary. The flavor is wonderfully intense.

INGREDIENTS

Serves 6
1 each red and yellow bell pepper
2 Spanish onions
2 large zucchini
1 large eggplant or 4 baby eggplant, trimmed
1 fennel bulb, thickly sliced
2 beefsteak tomatoes
8 fat garlic cloves
2 tbsp olive oil
fresh rosemary sprigs
black pepper
lemon wedges and black olives (optional), to garnish

1 Halve and seed the peppers, then cut them into large chunks. Peel the onions and cut into thick wedges.

NUTRITION NOTES

Per portion:	
Energy	120Kcals/504kJ
Fat	5.2g
Saturated fat	0.68g
Cholesterol	0

2 Cut the zucchini and eggplant into large chunks.

3 Preheat the oven to 425°F. Spread the peppers, onions, zucchini, eggplant and fennel in a lightly oiled shallow ovenproof dish or roasting pan, or, if desired, arrange in rows to make a colorful design.

4 Cut each tomato in half and place, cut-side up, with the vegetables.

5 Tuck the garlic cloves among the vegetables, then brush them with the olive oil. Place some sprigs of rosemary among the vegetables and grind some black pepper over the top, particularly on the tomatoes.

6 Roast for 20–25 minutes, turning the vegetables halfway through the cooking time. Serve from the dish or on a flat platter, garnished with lemon wedges. Scatter some black olives over the top, if desired.

VEGETABLES À LA GRECQUE

This simple side salad is made with winter vegetables, but you can vary it according to the season. This combination of vegetables makes an ideal, low fat side salad to serve with grilled lean meat or poultry, or with thick slices of fresh, crusty bread.

INGREDIENTS

Serves 4

¾ cup white wine
1 tsp olive oil
2 tbsp lemon juice
2 bay leaves
sprig of fresh thyme
4 juniper berries
1 lb leeks, cut into 1in lengths
1 small cauliflower, broken into florets
4 celery stalks, sliced on the diagonal
2 tbsp chopped fresh parsley
salt and black pepper

1 Put the wine, oil, lemon juice, bay leaves, thyme and juniper berries into a large, heavy saucepan and bring to a boil. Cover and let simmer for 20 minutes.

2 Add the leeks, cauliflower and celery. Simmer very gently for 5–6 minutes, or until just tender.

NUTRITION NOTES

Per portion:

Energy	88Kcals/368kJ
Protein	4.53g
Fat	2.05g
Saturated fat	0.11g
Fiber	4.42g

3 Remove the vegetables with a slotted spoon and transfer them to a serving dish. Briskly boil the cooking liquid for 15–20 minutes, or until reduced by half. Strain.

4 Stir the parsley into the liquid and season with salt and pepper to taste. Pour over the vegetables and allow to cool. Chill in the fridge for at least 1 hour before serving.

> COOK'S TIP
> Choose a dry or medium-dry white wine for best results.

GREEN PAPAYA SALAD

There are many variations of this salad in southeast Asia. Because green papaya is not easy to find, shredded carrots, cucumber or green apple may be substituted. Serve this salad with raw white cabbage and rice.

INGREDIENTS

Serves 4
1 medium green papaya
4 garlic cloves
1 tbsp chopped shallots
3–4 red chilies, seeded and sliced
½ tsp salt
2–3 green beans, cut into
  ¾ in lengths
2 tomatoes, cut into wedges
3 tbsp fish sauce
1 tbsp sugar
juice of 1 lime
2 tbsp crushed roasted peanuts
sliced red chilies, to garnish

1 Peel the papaya and cut in half lengthwise, scrape out the seeds with a spoon and finely shred the flesh.

2 Grind the garlic, shallots, chilies and salt together in a large mortar and pestle.

NUTRITION NOTES

Per portion:
Energy	96Kcals/402kJ
Fat	4.2g
Saturated fat	0.77g
Cholesterol	0

3 Add the shredded papaya a little at a time and pound until it becomes slightly limp and soft.

4 Add the sliced beans and tomatoes and lightly crush. Season with fish sauce, sugar and lime juice.

5 Transfer the salad to a serving dish, sprinkle with crushed peanuts and garnish with chilies.

COOK'S TIP
If you do not have a large mortar and pestle, use a bowl and crush the shredded papaya with a wooden meat pounder or the end of a rolling pin.

EGGPLANT SALAD

An appetizing and unusual salad that you will find yourself making over and over again.

INGREDIENTS

Serves 6

2 eggplant
1 tbsp oil
2 tbsp dried shrimp, soaked
   and drained
1 tbsp coarsely chopped garlic
2 tbsp fresh lime juice
1 tsp sugar
2 tbsp fish sauce
1 hard-cooked egg, chopped
4 shallots, thinly sliced into rings
cilantro leaves, to garnish
2 red chilies, seeded and sliced,
   to garnish

COOK'S TIP
For an interesting variation, if available, try using salted duck's or quail's eggs, cut in half, instead of chopped hen's eggs.

1 Grill or roast the eggplant until charred and tender.

2 When cool enough to handle, peel away the skin and slice the eggplant into thick pieces.

3 Heat the oil in a small frying pan, add the drained shrimp and the garlic and fry until golden. Remove from the pan and set aside.

4 To make the dressing, put the lime juice, sugar and fish sauce in a small bowl and whisk together.

5 To serve, arrange the eggplant on a serving dish. Top with the chopped egg, shallot rings and dried shrimp mixture. Drizzle on the dressing and garnish with cilantro and red chilies.

NUTRITION NOTES

Per portion:
Energy	70.5Kcals/295kJ
Fat	3.76g
Saturated fat	0.68g
Cholesterol	57mg
Fiber	1.20g

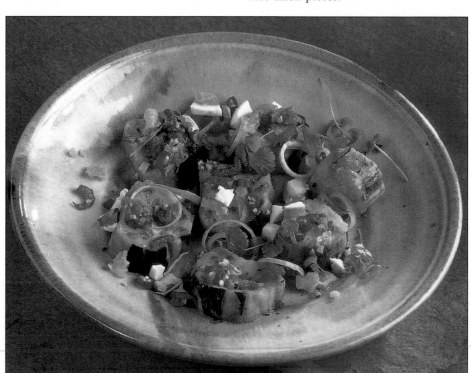

BAMBOO SHOOT SALAD

This salad, which has a hot and sharp flavor, originated in northeast Thailand. Use fresh young bamboo shoots if you can find them, otherwise substitute canned bamboo shoots.

INGREDIENTS

Serves 4
1 14oz can whole bamboo shoots
1oz glutinous rice
2 tbsp chopped shallots
1 tbsp chopped garlic
3 tbsp chopped scallions
2 tbsp fish sauce
2 tbsp lime juice
1 tsp sugar
½ tsp dried flaked chilies
20–25 small mint leaves
1 tbsp toasted sesame seeds

1 Rinse and drain the bamboo shoots, then slice and set aside.

2 Dry roast the rice in a frying pan until it is golden brown. Remove and grind to fine crumbs with a mortar and pestle.

3 Transfer the rice to a bowl, add the shallots, garlic, scallions, fish sauce, lime juice, sugar, chilies and half the mint leaves.

COOK'S TIP
Omit the sesame seeds to reduce calories and fat. Use prepared minced garlic instead of crushing your own.

4 Mix thoroughly, then add the bamboo shoots and toss together. Serve sprinkled with sesame seeds and the remaining mint leaves.

NUTRITION NOTES

Per portion:

Energy	73.5Kcals/308kJ
Fat	2.8g
Saturated fat	0.41g
Cholesterol	0
Fiber	2.45g

FRUIT AND FIBER SALAD

Fresh, fast and filling, this salad makes a great supper or snack.

INGREDIENTS

Serves 6

8oz red or white cabbage, or a mixture of both
3 medium carrots
1 pear
1 red-skinned eating apple
1 7oz can cannellini beans, drained
¼ cup chopped dates

For the dressing
½ tsp dry English mustard
2 tsp honey
2 tbsp orange juice
1 tsp white wine vinegar
½ tsp paprika
salt and black pepper

1 Shred the cabbage very finely, discarding the core and tough ribs.

2 Cut the carrots into very thin strips, about 2in long.

3 Quarter, core and slice the pear and the apple, leaving the peel on.

4 Put the fruit and vegetables in a bowl with the beans and dates. Mix well.

5 To make the dressing, blend the mustard with the honey until smooth. Add the orange juice, vinegar, paprika and seasoning and mix well.

6 Pour the dressing over the salad and toss to coat. Chill in the fridge for 30 minutes before serving.

NUTRITION NOTES

Per portion:
Energy	137Kcals/574kJ
Fat	0.87g
Saturated fat	0.03g
Fiber	6.28g

COOK'S TIP

Use other canned beans, such as red kidney beans or chickpeas, in place of the cannellini beans. Add ½ tsp ground spice, such as chili powder, cumin or coriander, for extra flavor. Add 1 tsp finely grated orange or lemon rind to the dressing, for extra flavor.

BULGUR SALAD WITH ORANGES

Bulgur makes an excellent alternative to rice or pasta.

INGREDIENTS

Serves 6
1 small green bell pepper
1 cup bulgur
½ cucumber, diced
½ cup chopped fresh mint
⅓ cup flaked almonds, toasted
grated rind and juice of 1 lemon
2 seedless oranges
salt and black pepper
mint sprigs, to garnish

1 Using a sharp vegetable knife, carefully halve and seed the green pepper. Cut it on a board into small cubes and put to one side.

2 Place the bulgur in a saucepan and add 2½ cups water. Bring to a boil, lower the heat, cover and simmer for 10–15 minutes, until tender. Alternatively, place the bulgur in a heatproof bowl, add boiling water and allow to soak for 30 minutes. Most, if not all, of the water should be absorbed; drain off any excess.

3 Toss the bulgur with the cucumber, green pepper, mint and toasted almonds in a serving bowl. Add the grated lemon rind and juice.

4 Cut the rind from the oranges, then working over the bowl to catch the juice, cut the oranges into neat segments. Add to the bulgur mixture, then season and toss lightly. Garnish with the mint sprigs.

NUTRITION NOTES	
Per portion:	
Energy	160Kcals/672kJ
Fat	4.3g
Saturated fat	0.33g
Cholesterol	0

BROWN RICE SALAD WITH FRUIT

An Asian-style dressing gives this colorful rice salad extra piquancy. Whole grains like brown rice are unrefined, so they retain their natural fiber, vitamins and minerals.

INGREDIENTS

Serves 4–6
⅔ cup brown rice
1 small red bell pepper, seeded and diced
1 7oz can corn niblets, drained
3 tbsp golden raisins
1 8oz can pineapple pieces in juice
1 tbsp light soy sauce
1 tsp sunflower oil
2 tsp hazelnut oil
1 garlic clove, crushed
1 tsp minced fresh ginger
ground black pepper
4 scallions, sliced, to garnish

COOK'S TIP
Hazelnut oil, which contains mainly monounsaturated fats, adds a wonderful flavor.

1 Cook the brown rice in a large saucepan of lightly salted boiling water for about 30 minutes, or until it is tender. Drain thoroughly and cool. Meanwhile, prepare the garnish by slicing the scallions at an angle and setting aside.

2 Transfer the rice to a bowl and add the red pepper, corn and raisins. Drain the pineapple pieces, reserving the juice, add them to the rice mixture and toss lightly.

3 Pour the reserved pineapple juice into a clean screw-top jar. Add the soy sauce, sunflower and hazelnut oils, garlic and ginger. Add some salt and pepper, then close the jar tightly and shake well to combine.

4 Pour the dressing over the salad and toss well. Sprinkle the scallions over the top.

NUTRITION NOTES	
Per portion:	
Energy	245Kcals/1029kJ
Fat	4.25g
Saturated fat	0.6g
Cholesterol	0

CRAB PASTA SALAD

Low fat yogurt makes a piquant dressing for this salad.

INGREDIENTS

Serves 6

12oz pasta twists
1 small red bell pepper, seeded and
  finely chopped
2 6oz cans white crabmeat, drained
4oz cherry tomatoes, halved
1/4 cucumber, halved, seeded and sliced
  into crescents
1 tbsp lemon juice
1 1/4 cups low fat yogurt
2 celery stalks, finely chopped
2 tsp creamed horseradish
1/2 tsp paprika
1/2 tsp Dijon mustard
2 tbsp sweet tomato pickle
  or chutney
salt and black pepper
fresh basil, to garnish

1 Cook the pasta in a large pot of boiling, salted water, according to the instructions on the package, until *al dente*. Drain and rinse thoroughly under cold water.

2 Cover the chopped red pepper with boiling water and allow to stand for 1 minute. Drain and rinse under cold water. Pat dry with paper towels.

NUTRITION NOTES

Per portion:

Energy	305Kcals/1283kJ
Fat	2.5g
Saturated fat	0.5g
Cholesterol	43mg
Fiber	2.9g

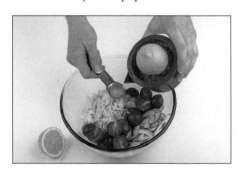

3 Drain the crabmeat and pick over carefully for pieces of shell. Put into a bowl with the halved tomatoes and sliced cucumber. Season with salt and pepper and sprinkle with lemon juice.

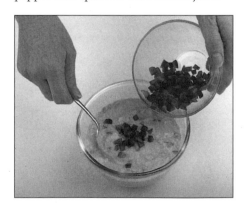

4 To make the dressing, add the red pepper to the yogurt, with the celery, creamed horseradish, paprika, mustard and sweet tomato pickle or chutney. Mix the pasta with the dressing and transfer to a serving dish. Spoon the crab mixture on top and garnish with fresh basil.

CACHUMBAR

Cachumbar is a salad relish most commonly served with Indian curries. There are many versions; this one will leave your mouth feeling cool and fresh after a spicy meal.

INGREDIENTS

Serves 4
3 ripe tomatoes
2 chopped scallions
¼ tsp sugar
salt
3 tbsp chopped fresh cilantro

NUTRITION NOTES

Per portion:

Energy	9.5Kcals/73.5kJ
Fat	0.23g
Saturated fat	0.07g
Cholesterol	0
Fiber	0.87g

1 Remove the tough cores from the bottom of the tomatoes with a small sharp-pointed knife.

> COOK'S TIP
> Cachumbar also makes a fine accompaniment to fresh crab, lobster and shellfish.

2 Halve the tomatoes, remove the seeds and dice the flesh.

3 Combine the tomatoes with the scallions, sugar, salt and chopped cilantro. Serve at room temperature.

DESSERTS

FILO CHIFFON PIE

Filo pastry is low in fat and is very easy to use. Keep a package in the freezer, ready to make impressive desserts like this one.

INGREDIENTS

Serves 6
1¼ lb rhubarb
1 tsp pumpkin pie spice
finely grated rind and juice of 1 orange
1 tbsp granulated sugar
1 tbsp butter
3 filo pastry sheets

1 Preheat the oven to 400°F. Wash the rhubarb, then trim and cut it into 1in pieces and put them in a bowl.

2 Add the pumpkin pie spice, orange rind and juice and sugar. Transfer the rhubarb to a 4-cup pie dish.

NUTRITION NOTES

Per portion:	
Energy	71Kcals/299kJ
Fat	2.5g
Saturated fat	1.41g
Cholesterol	5.74mg
Fiber	1.48g

3 Melt the butter and brush it over the pastry. Lift the pastry onto the pie dish, butter-side up, and crumple it up decoratively to cover the pie.

> VARIATION
> Other fruit can be used in this pie – just prepare depending on type.

4 Put the dish on a baking sheet and bake for 20 minutes, until golden brown. Reduce the heat to 350°F and bake for another 10–15 minutes, until the rhubarb is tender.

Blushing Pears

Pears poached in rosé wine and sweet spices absorb all the subtle flavors and turn a delightful soft pink color.

Serves 6
6 firm eating pears
1¼ cups rosé wine
⅔ cup cranberry or
   clear apple juice
strip of thinly pared orange rind
1 cinnamon stick
4 whole cloves
1 bay leaf
5 tbsp sugar
small bay leaves, to decorate

1 Thinly peel the pears with a sharp knife or vegetable peeler, leaving the stalks attached.

2 Pour the wine and cranberry or apple juice into a large heavy saucepan. Add the orange rind, cinnamon stick, cloves, bay leaf and sugar.

3 Heat gently, stirring all the time, until the sugar has dissolved. Add the pears and stand them upright in the pan. Pour in enough cold water to barely cover them. Cover and cook gently for 20–30 minutes, or until just tender, turning and basting occasionally.

4 Using a slotted spoon, gently lift the pears out of the syrup and transfer to a serving dish.

5 Bring the syrup to a boil and boil rapidly for 10–15 minutes, or until it has reduced by half.

6 Strain the syrup and pour over the pears. Serve hot or well-chilled, decorated with small bay leaves.

Nutrition Notes	
Per portion:	
Energy	148Kcals/620kJ
Fat	0.16g
Saturated fat	0
Fiber	2.93g

COOK'S TIP
Check the pears by piercing with a skewer or sharp knife toward the end of the poaching time, because some may cook more quickly than others. Serve immediately, or allow to cool in the syrup and then chill.

Baked Apples in Honey and Lemon

A classic mix of flavors in a healthy, traditional family dessert. Serve warm, with skim-milk pudding or low fat frozen yogurt.

Ingredients

Serves 4

4 medium cooking apples
1 tbsp honey
grated rind and juice of 1 lemon
1 tbsp low fat margarine
low fat frozen yogurt, to serve

1 Preheat the oven to 350°F. Remove the cores from the apples, leaving them whole.

Nutrition Notes

Per portion:
Energy	61Kcals/259.5kJ
Fat	1.62g
Saturated fat	0.42g
Cholesterol	0.25mg

2 With a sharp knife, cut lines through the apple skin at intervals, then arrange the apples in an oven-proof dish.

3 Combine the honey, lemon rind, juice and low fat margarine.

4 Spoon the mixture into the apples and cover the dish with foil or a lid. Bake for 40–45 minutes, or until the apples are tender. Serve with frozen yogurt.

APPLE AND BLACK CURRANT PANCAKES

These pancakes are made with a whole-wheat batter and are filled with a delicious fruit mixture.

INGREDIENTS

Makes 10

1 cup whole-wheat flour

1¼ cups skim milk

1 egg, beaten

1 tbsp sunflower oil, plus extra for greasing

low fat crème fraîche, to serve (optional)

toasted nuts or sesame seeds, for sprinkling (optional)

For the filling

1 lb cooking apples

8oz black currants

2–3 tbsp water

2 tbsp raw sugar

1 To make the pancake batter, put the flour in a mixing bowl and make a well in the center.

2 Add a little of the milk with the egg and the oil. Beat the flour into the liquid, then gradually beat in the rest of the milk, keeping the batter smooth and free from lumps. Cover the batter and chill while you prepare the filling.

3 Quarter, peel and core the apples. Slice them into a pan and add the black currants and water. Cook over low heat for 10–15 minutes until the fruit is soft. Stir in enough raw sugar to sweeten.

4 Lightly grease a nonstick pan with just a smear of oil. Heat the pan, pour in about 2 tablespoons of the batter, swirl it around and cook for about 1 minute. Flip the pancake over with a spatula and cook the other side. Put on a piece of paper towel and keep hot while cooking the remaining pancakes.

5 Fill the pancakes with the apple and black currant mixture and roll them up. Serve with a dollop of crème fraîche, if using, and sprinkle with nuts or sesame seeds, if desired.

COOK'S TIP

If you wish, substitute other combinations of fruit for apples and black currants.

NUTRITION NOTES

Per portion:

Energy	120Kcals/505kJ
Fat	3g
Saturated fat	0.5g
Cholesterol	25mg

RASPBERRY VACHERIN

Meringue rounds filled with orange-flavored low fat cream cheese and fresh raspberries make this a perfect dinner party dessert.

INGREDIENTS

Serves 6
3 egg whites
¾ cup superfine sugar
1 tsp chopped almonds
confectioners' sugar, for dusting
raspberry leaves, to decorate (optional)

For the filling
¾ cup low fat cream cheese
1–2 tbsp honey
1–2 tbsp Cointreau
½ cup low fat ricotta
   or farmer's cheese
8oz raspberries

NUTRITION NOTES
Per portion:

Energy	197Kcals/837.5kJ
Fat	1.02g
Saturated fat	0.36g
Cholesterol	1.67mg
Fiber	1g

COOK'S TIP
When making the meringue, whisk the egg whites until they are so stiff that you can turn the bowl upside-down without their falling out.

1 Preheat the oven to 275°F. Draw an 8in circle on two pieces of non-stick parchment paper. Turn the paper over so the marking is on the underside and use it to line two heavy baking sheets.

2 Whisk the egg whites in a clean bowl until very stiff, then gradually whisk in the superfine sugar to make a stiff meringue mixture.

3 Spoon the mixture onto the circles on the prepared baking sheets, spreading the meringue evenly to the edges. Sprinkle one meringue round with the chopped almonds.

4 Bake for 1½–2 hours or until crisp and dry, then carefully lift the meringue rounds off the baking sheets. Peel away the paper and cool the meringues on a wire rack.

5 To make the filling, cream the soft cheese with the honey and liqueur in a bowl. Gradually fold in the ricotta cheese and the raspberries, reserving three berries for decoration.

6 Place the plain meringue round on a board, spread with the filling and top with the nut-covered round. Dust with the confectioners' sugar, transfer to a serving plate and decorate with the reserved raspberries and a sprig of raspberry leaves, if desired.

COOL GREEN FRUIT SALAD

A sophisticated, simple fruit salad for any time of year.

INGREDIENTS

Serves 6

3 cantaloupes
4oz green seedless grapes
2 kiwi fruit
1 star fruit
1 green-skinned eating apple
1 lime
¾ cup sparkling grape juice

NUTRITION NOTES

Per portion:

Energy	67Kcals/285kJ
Fat	0.27g
Saturated fat	0
Cholesterol	0
Fiber	1.22g

1 Cut the melons in half and scoop out the seeds. Keeping the shells intact, scoop out the fruit with a melon baller, or scoop it out with a spoon and cut into bite-size cubes. Set aside the melon shells.

> COOK'S TIP
> If you're serving this dessert on a hot summer day, serve the filled melon shells nestling on a platter of crushed ice to keep them beautifully cool.

2 Remove any stems from the grapes and, if they are large, cut them in half. Peel and chop the kiwi fruit. Thinly slice the star fruit. Core and thinly slice the apple and place the slices in a bowl with the melon, grapes, kiwi fruit and star fruit.

3 Thinly pare the rind from the lime and cut it into fine strips. Blanch the strips in boiling water for 30 seconds, then drain them and rinse in cold water. Squeeze the juice from the lime and toss it into the fruit. Mix gently.

4 Spoon the prepared fruit into the melon shells and chill in the fridge until required. Just before serving, spoon the sparkling grape juice over the fruit and sprinkle it with the blanched lime rind.

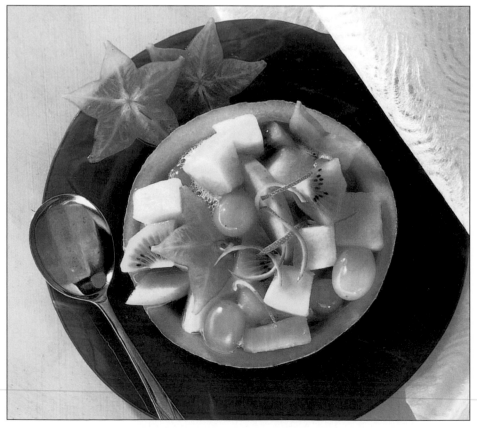

ICED ORANGES

The ultimate fat-free treat –
these delectable orange sherbets
served in fruit shells were
originally sold in beach cafes
in the south of France.

INGREDIENTS

Serves 8
⅔ *cup sugar*
juice of 1 lemon
14 medium oranges
8 fresh bay leaves, to decorate

NUTRITION NOTES

Per portion:

Energy	139Kcals/593kJ
Fat	0.17g
Saturated fat	0
Cholesterol	0
Fiber	3g

COOK'S TIP
Use crumpled paper towels to
keep the shells upright.

1 Put the sugar in a heavy saucepan.
Add half the lemon juice, then add
½ cup water. Cook over low heat until
the sugar has dissolved. Bring to a boil
and boil for 2–3 minutes, until the
syrup is clear.

2 Slice the tops off eight of the
oranges to make "hats." Scoop out
the flesh of the oranges and reserve.
Freeze the empty orange shells and
"hats" until needed.

3 Grate the rind of the remaining
oranges and add to the syrup.
Squeeze the juice from the oranges,
and from the reserved flesh. There
should be 3 cups. Squeeze another
orange or add bought orange juice,
if necessary.

4 Stir the orange juice and remaining
lemon juice, with 6 tablespoons
water, into the syrup. Taste, adding
more lemon juice or sugar as desired.
Pour the mixture into a shallow freezer
container and freeze for 3 hours.

5 Turn the orange sherbet mixture
into a bowl and whisk thoroughly
to break up the ice crystals. Freeze for
4 hours more, until firm, but not solid.

6 Pack the mixture into the hollowed-
out orange shells, mounding it up,
and set the "hats" on top. Freeze the
sherbet shells until ready to serve. Just
before serving, make a hole with a
skewer in the tops of the "hats" and
push in a bay leaf, to decorate.

Yogurt Sundaes with Passionfruit

Here is a sundae you can enjoy every day! The frozen yogurt has less fat and fewer calories than traditional ice cream, and the fruits provide vitamins A and C.

INGREDIENTS

Serves 4

*12oz strawberries, hulled
and halved*
2 passionfruit, halved
2 tsp confectioners' sugar
2 ripe peaches, pitted and chopped
*8 scoops (about 12oz) vanilla or
strawberry frozen yogurt*

COOK'S TIP
Choose reduced-fat or virtually fat-free frozen yogurt or ice cream, to cut the calories and fat.

---

1 Purée half the strawberries. Scoop out the passionfruit pulp and add it to the sauce. Sweeten, if necessary.

NUTRITION NOTES

Per portion:
Energy	135Kcals/560kJ
Fat	1g
Saturated fat	0.5g
Cholesterol	3.5mg

---

2 Spoon half the remaining strawberries and half the chopped peaches into four tall sundae glasses. Top each dessert with a scoop of frozen yogurt. Set aside a few choice pieces of fruit for decoration, and use the rest to make another layer on the top of each sundae. Top each sundae with a final scoop of frozen yogurt.

3 Top with the passionfruit sauce and decorate the sundaes with the remaining strawberries and pieces of peach. Serve immediately.

Fruit Fondue with Hazelnut Dip

INGREDIENTS

Serves 2

*selection of fresh fruit for dipping, such
as clementines, figs, apricots, grapes,
nectarines and plums*
½ cup reduced fat cream cheese
1¼ cup low fat hazelnut yogurt
1 tsp vanilla extract
1 tsp sugar

NUTRITION NOTES

Per portion (dip only):
Energy	170Kcals/714kJ
Fat	4g
Saturated fat	2.5g
Cholesterol	6.5mg

---

1 First prepare the fruit. Peel and segment the clementines, removing as much of the white pith as possible. Quarter the fresh figs and apricots, wash the grapes and slice the nectarines and plums.

2 Beat the cream cheese with the yogurt, vanilla extract and sugar in a bowl. Spoon the mixture into a glass serving dish set on a platter or into small dishes on individual plates.

3 Arrange the prepared fruits around the dip and serve immediately.

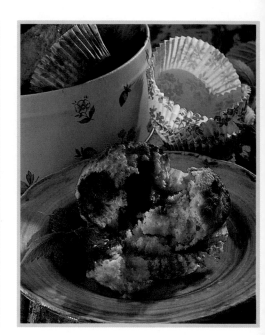

CAKES,
BAKES &
COOKIES

~

ANGEL CAKE

This cake makes a delicious light dessert, served on its own or with fresh fruit.

INGREDIENTS

Serves 10
¹/₃ cup cornstarch
¹/₃ cup all-purpose flour
8 egg whites
1 cup superfine sugar, plus extra for
 sprinkling
1 tsp vanilla extract
confectioners' sugar, for dusting

1 Preheat the oven to 350°F. Sift the flour and the cornstarch onto a sheet of wax paper.

2 Whisk the egg whites in a large, clean, dry bowl until very stiff, then gradually add the sugar and vanilla extract, whisking until the mixture is thick and glossy.

3 Gently fold in the flour mixture with a large metal spoon. Spoon into an ungreased 10-inch angel cake pan, smooth the surface and bake for about 45–50 minutes, or until the cake springs back when lightly pressed.

COOK'S TIP
Low fat cream cheese and fresh fruit are the ideal complement to this cake.

4 Sprinkle a piece of wax paper with sugar and set an egg cup in the center. Invert the cake pan over the paper, balancing it carefully on the egg cup. When cold, the cake will drop out of the tin. Transfer it to a plate, decorate, if desired, then dust with confectioners' sugar and serve.

NUTRITION NOTES	
Per portion:	
Energy	139Kcals/582kJ
Fat	0.08g
Saturated fat	0.01g
Cholesterol	0
Fiber	0.13g

TIA MARIA SPONGE CAKE

A feather-light coffee sponge with a creamy liqueur-flavored filling.

───── INGREDIENTS ─────

Serves 8
¾ cup all-purpose flour
2 tbsp instant coffee powder
3 eggs
½ cup superfine sugar
coffee beans, to decorate (optional)

For the filling
¾ cup low fat cream cheese
1 tbsp honey
1 tbsp Tia Maria liqueur
¼ cup preserved ginger,
  coarsely chopped

For the icing
1¾ cups confectioners' sugar, sifted
2 tsp coffee extract
1 tbsp water
1 tsp reduced-fat cocoa powder

───── NUTRITION NOTES ─────

Per portion:
Energy   226Kcals/951kJ
Fat   3.14g
Saturated fat   1.17g
Cholesterol   75.03mg
Fiber   0.64g

COOK'S TIP
When folding in the flour mixture, take care not to beat out all the air, as it helps the cake to rise.

1 Preheat the oven to 375°F. Grease and line an 8-inch deep round cake pan. Sift the flour and coffee powder together onto a sheet of wax paper.

2 Whisk the eggs and sugar in a bowl with a hand-held electric whisk until thick and mousse-like. (When the whisk is lifted, a trail should remain on the surface of the mixture for at least 15 seconds.)

3 Gently fold in the flour mixture with a rubber spatula. Turn the mixture into the prepared pan. Bake for 30–35 minutes or until it springs back when lightly pressed. Turn onto a wire rack to cool completely.

4 To make the filling, mix the soft cheese with the honey in a bowl. Beat until smooth, then stir in the Tia Maria and chopped stem ginger.

5 Split the cake in half horizontally and sandwich the two halves together with the Tia Maria filling.

6 Make the icing. In a bowl, mix the confectioners' sugar and coffee extract with enough water to make a consistency that will coat the back of a wooden spoon. Pour three-quarters of the icing over the cake, spreading it evenly to the edges. Stir the cocoa into the remaining icing until smooth. Spoon into a pastry bag fitted with a writing nozzle and pipe the mocha icing over the coffee icing. Decorate with coffee beans, if desired.

RASPBERRY MUFFINS

These muffins are made using baking powder and low fat buttermilk, giving them a light and spongy texture. They are delicious to eat at any time of the day.

INGREDIENTS

Makes 10–12

2½ cups all-purpose flour
1 tbsp baking powder
½ cup superfine sugar
1 egg
1 cup buttermilk
4 tbsp sunflower oil
5oz raspberries

NUTRITION NOTES

Per portion:

Energy	171Kcals/719kJ
Fat	4.55g
Saturated fat	0.71g
Cholesterol	16.5mg
Fiber	1.02g

1 Preheat the oven to 400°F. Arrange 12 paper cases in a deep muffin pan. Sift the flour and baking powder into a mixing bowl, stir in the sugar, then make a well in the center.

2 Mix the egg, buttermilk and sunflower oil together in a bowl, pour into the flour mixture and mix quickly.

3 Add the raspberries and lightly fold in with a rubber spatula. Spoon the mixture into the paper cases.

4 Bake the muffins for 20–25 minutes, until golden brown and firm in the middle. Transfer to a wire rack and serve warm or cold.

DATE AND APPLE MUFFINS

You will only need one or two of these wholesome muffins per person, because they are very filling.

INGREDIENTS

Makes 12

1¼ cups self-rising whole-wheat flour
1¼ cups self-rising white flour
1 tsp ground cinnamon
1 tsp baking powder
2 tbsp soft margarine
½ cup light brown sugar
1 apple
1 cup apple juice
2 tbsp pear and apple spread
1 egg, lightly beaten
½ cup chopped dates
1 tbsp chopped pecans

1 Preheat the oven to 400°F. Arrange 12 paper cases in a deep muffin tin. Put the whole-wheat flour in a mixing bowl. Sift in the white flour with the cinnamon and baking powder. Rub in the margarine until the mixture resembles bread crumbs, then stir in the brown sugar.

NUTRITION NOTES

Per portion:

Energy	163Kcals/686kJ
Fat	2.98g
Saturated fat	0.47g
Cholesterol	16.04mg
Fiber	1.97g

2 Quarter and core the apple, chop the flesh finely and set aside. Stir a little of the apple juice with the pear and apple spread until smooth. Mix in the remaining juice, then add to the rubbed-in mixture with the egg. Add the chopped apple to the bowl with the dates. Mix quickly until just combined.

COOK'S TIP
Pear and apple spread is a highly concentrated paste. It is available in health food stores. You can substitute apple butter, but the flavor will not be as intense.

3 Divide the mixture among the muffin cases.

4 Sprinkle with the chopped pecans. Bake the muffins for 20–25 minutes, until golden brown and firm in the middle. Remove to a wire rack and serve while still warm.

CINNAMON APPLE GÂTEAU

Make this lovely cake for an autumn celebration.

INGREDIENTS

Serves 8
3 eggs
1/2 cup sugar
3/4 cup all-purpose flour
1 tsp ground cinnamon

For the filling and topping
4 large eating apples
4 tbsp honey
1 tbsp water
1/2 cup golden raisins
1/2 tsp ground cinnamon
1 1/2 cups low fat cream cheese
4 tbsp reduced fat ricotta cheese
2 tsp lemon juice
3 tbsp apricot glaze
mint sprig, to decorate

1 Preheat the oven to 375°F. Grease and line a 9 in layer cake pan. Place the eggs and sugar in a bowl and beat with a hand-held electric whisk until thick and mousse-like. (When the whisk is lifted, a trail should remain on the surface of the mixture for at least 15 seconds.)

NUTRITION NOTES

Per portion:	
Energy	244Kcals/1023kJ
Fat	4.05g
Saturated fat	1.71g
Cholesterol	77.95mg
Fiber	1.50g

2 Sift the flour and cinnamon over the egg mixture and fold in with a rubber spatula. Pour into the prepared pan and bake for 25–30 minutes or until the cake springs back when lightly pressed. Turn the cake onto a wire rack to cool.

3 To make the filling, peel, core and slice three of the apples and put them in a saucepan. Add 2 tbsp of the honey and the water. Cover and cook over gentle heat for about 10 minutes. Add the raisins and cinnamon, stir well, replace the lid and let cool.

4 Put the cream cheese in a bowl with the remaining honey, the ricotta cheese and half the lemon juice. Beat until the mixture is smooth.

5 Halve the cake horizontally, place the bottom half on a board and drizzle over any liquid from the apples. Spread with two-thirds of the cheese mixture, then top with the apple filling. Fit the top of the cake in place.

6 Swirl the remaining cheese mixture over the top of the cake. Core and slice the remaining apple, sprinkle with lemon juice and use to decorate the edge of the cake. Brush the apple with the apricot glaze and place mint sprigs on top, to decorate.

COOK'S TIP
Apricot glaze is useful for brushing over any kind of fresh fruit topping or filling. Place a few spoonfuls of apricot jam in a small pan along with a squeeze of lemon juice. Heat the jam, stirring until it is melted and runny. Pour the melted jam into a wire strainer set over a bowl. Stir the jam with a wooden spoon to help it go through. Return the strained jam to the pan. Keep the glaze warm until needed.

OATY CRISPS

These cookies are very crisp and crunchy – ideal to serve with morning coffee.

INGREDIENTS

Makes 18
1¾ cups rolled oats
½ cup light brown sugar
1 egg
4 tbsp sunflower oil
2 tbsp malt extract

NUTRITION NOTES

Per portion:
Energy	86Kcals/360kJ
Fat	3.59g
Saturated fat	0.57g
Cholesterol	10.7mg
Fiber	0.66g

1 Preheat the oven to 375°F. Lightly grease two baking sheets. Mix the rolled oats and sugar in a bowl, breaking up any lumps in the sugar. Add the egg, sunflower oil and malt extract, mix well, then allow to soak for 15 minutes.

2 Using a teaspoon, place small heaps of the mixture well apart on the prepared baking sheets. Press the heaps into 3-inch rounds with the back of a dampened fork.

3 Bake the cookies for 10–15 minutes until golden brown. Let them cool for 1 minute, then remove with a spatula and cool on a wire rack.

COOK'S TIP
Malt extract, a flavoring, isn't widely available; look for it in health-food stores. If you can't find malt extract, you can substitute maple extract, but the flavor is different.

DROP SCONES

These little scones are delicious spread with jam.

INGREDIENTS

Makes 18
2 cups self-rising flour
½ tsp salt
1 tbsp sugar
1 egg, beaten
1¼ cups skim milk
oil, for frying

1 Preheat a griddle, heavy frying pan or an electric frying pan. Sift the flour and salt into a mixing bowl. Stir in the sugar and make a well in the center.

2 Add the egg and half the milk, then gradually incorporate the surrounding flour to make a smooth batter. Beat in the remaining milk.

3 Lightly oil the griddle or pan. Drop tablespoons of the batter onto the surface, leaving them until they bubble and the bubbles begin to burst.

NUTRITION NOTES

Per portion:
Energy	64Kcals/270kJ
Fat	1.09g
Saturated fat	0.2g
Cholesterol	11.03mg
Fiber	0.43g

4 Turn the drop scones over with a spatula and cook until the underside is golden brown. Keep the cooked drop scones warm and moist by wrapping them in a clean napkin while cooking successive batches.

> **COOK'S TIP**
> For savory scones, add 2 chopped scallions and 1 tbsp freshly grated Parmesan cheese. Serve with cottage cheese.

INDEX